Understanding the Law of Abundance

GW00566974

Ignorance is blindness. An in-depth understanding of spiritual law is beyond the comprehension of the human mind.

Andrew Abraham

DEDICATION

This book is dedicated to God Almighty. The creator of all things, both visible and invisible.

CONTENTS

Introduction

Laws govern everything visible and invisible; existence itself is sustained by them. Likewise, to succeed and live a life of abundance, you need to carefully obey certain laws: the laws of abundance.

For a student to pass an examination, specific laws must be followed. First must attend lectures and then must study what has been taught. Nothing happens by accident. Everything has its own laws that must be followed to function effectively. You may have wondered why some people are successful in life, especially if you haven't witnessed them obeying any significant laws indicative of success. At this juncture, it is important to remember that the Divine does not discriminate. Some people who actually experience abundance are unconsciously obeying divine laws that trigger abundance.

Some people may still be thirsty after a great, rainy day. Why? After all, hasn't it just rained? The answer is simple: they fail to follow the principles of water storage. Regardless of the amount of rainfall, if you fail to store the water and instead allow all of it to waste, you may suffer thirst the following day. This principle is applicable to all areas of life.

To ensure that you enjoy abundance in life, you must obey laws that govern abundance. That is the purpose of this book. The idea of

i

abundance is not restricted to financial gain but covers all aspects of life, including good health, peace, and blessings. It is about not taking anything for granted. It is about stopping and looking around you, and simply appreciating the feel of your feet on the ground and the sun brightening the world around you.

But there is more to the concept than meets the eye.

This book is an attempt to enlighten you on the existing laws that will open supernatural doors for you to perpetually walk in the realm of abundance. I am aware that ignorance can cause pain and grief. Therefore, I have carefully defined various laws that you may need to know that will help develop your knowledge and enhance your understanding on spiritual matters that are important for a colorful living.

Every chapter in this book covers several laws, and, at the end of each chapter, I also offer a few steps that you should follow to better appreciate each law and set in motion the law of abundance.

In this book, I looked at the laws that govern man and his reality. I looked at these laws under three headings:

- Spiritual law
- Natural law and
- Manmade law

I will be looking at these laws in depth in chapter 1.

Among the laws I examined, spiritual law is the most real and powerful. In fact, spiritual law influences both natural and manmade law, concurrently controlling the natural and physical realms. The laws of nature and mankind are the offspring of spiritual law and could not exist without it. And spiritual force is the power that sets spiritual law in motion.

Every law on earth is set in motion by a force, and the force behind every law takes its root from the spirit realm. This means that the spirit world exacts its force and influence on the natural world. Jesus said in the Lord's Prayer, "Let thy will be done on earth as it is in heaven."

The will of God is unseen. It is mandatory that the *will* of God will manifest here (the natural realm). This obviously suggests to us that everything happening here on earth is determined and masterminded in the unseen realm. So, everything we experience on earth today is directly influenced and manipulated in the spirit world, which has its own laws. For instance, the amount of wealth and sustenance you have amassed today can be attributed to what heaven has specifically allowed for you. "A man can receive nothing except it is given to him from above."

If this is true, man's fortune and his very existence are determined by the spirit world, and we know that the spirit does not discriminate. It is therefore wise to ask: Why are some people so wealthy, living lives of abundance, while others are poor? Why do some have cars and houses while others have neither? Why do some eat the most choice meals while others barely have something to eat? I believe this is the question many are asking today. I once heard someone say that God is unfair. But is *that* fair to say, or is it possible that the problem is man-made? This book will examine these mysteries of life to enlighten you on spiritual matters that will bring you greater abundance.

Every society in our world has a government, lines of authority, and laws that govern the people. Violations of laid-down societal laws are punishable in accordance with penalties defined by the overseeing authorities. For instance, in the UK, where I live, the judiciary branch enacts laws, which are administered by the police and other enforcement agencies. All living on the island must obey its laws; it is the same for visitors, irrespective of their country of origin or the length of their stay. All drivers, for instance, must stop when the traffic light turns red. You cannot say, "Well, I am only visiting the country, so I am not required by law to obey traffic lights, because the country I came from doesn't have traffic lights."

There is always some form of punishment attached to the violation of laws, whether spiritual or natural. This is true in all senses. Nobody is exempt from paying tax, for instance. We have heard of many businessmen who have been sent to prison and had their assets confiscated to mitigate their tax liabilities after they attempted to evade paying. Likewise, the failure to keep the law of abundance and financial obligations demanded by spiritual laws also has consequences.

Every man has equal opportunity to succeed and obtain peace, but not all people live successful lives—some live horrible ones. Some are born with more than others, but that doesn't mean we don't all have the capability of earning the life we want.

To attract wealth and abundance, a person must be able to harmonize spiritual and natural laws to his or her advantage. To feel the floor beneath his feet and the sun upon them. After reading this book, the way to live a life of blessings and abundance will become obvious to you.

ANDREW ABRAHAM

1
Laws

All things animate and inanimate, visible and invisible, are governed by laws that dictate their function and existence.

Laws are very important, and they control everything. Factors visible and invisible depend on them for existence. For laws to function effectively, they must be obeyed. Without

1

laws, there would be no form nor shape and neither would there be existence. Just imagine a society without laws, without government. Obviously, nobody would survive. Even criminals have their own rules that help their groups function harmoniously and achieve a common objective. Each home has its own laws. Every mother or father, regardless of parenting ability, expects a certain type of conduct and behavior from children.

God created the universe and set laws in motion to give meaning to His creation. In accordance with the laws of the land, there are behaviors that are considered acceptable and not acceptable in every society. Likewise, business corporations have their own business ethics and standard behaviors they expect from their employees. Before there can be conformity to expected behavior, there must be laws in place that define what is expected.

Laws give form and existence to everything spiritual and physical. Billions of birds of different kinds fly in the air. Interestingly, even without traffic lights or traffic wardens regulating their use of airspace, they don't bump into each other. They know when to retire for rest along with what to eat and not to eat, and they can spot danger and stay away from it. Birds are able to do all this because they understand and obey the laws that govern each activity.

A harmonious state can be achieved only when we comply with laws. A state of harmony is a state of bliss between you and your environment. The violation of laws can deny you bliss, which in turn can engender a negative effect on your well-being. The effects of violating laws may be subtle, yet they can also be fatal, as your actions may alter the harmony between you and nature. The outbreak of diseases represents one example of what stems from man's attempts to alter nature by forcing it to abandon its original course and take on another. Some examples of such attempts include the killing of unwanted children through abortion, animal crossbreeding, and genetically modified food.

Man is the cause of his state of being in every sense. It is often said that man is the architect of his own fortune and misfortune. Each decision delivers consequence. Karma is a spiritual principle that stipulates that whatever we sow, we will reap. This principle cannot be altered, because it is the law. Compliance to law ushers in a golden key that opens an invisible door to blessings and abundance. Compliance can be summed up in one word: *obedience*. There are rewards for obedience, and, likewise, punishment for disobedience.

Laws can be categorized under three headings: spiritual law, natural law, and man-made law. To enjoy bliss and abundance, you must be able to harmonize these laws to your advantage. One law cannot impair or violate the function of another law. They must work in unison for you to command blessings and abundance. However, a superior law can supersede a lesser one. For instance, if you get away with murder in a court of law, you will not be able to avoid the karmic repercussion that follows your deed based on the spiritual law that says "thou shalt not kill." However, this karma can be atoned for over time if you confess your sin, ask for forgiveness, and repent. If you begin doing what is right and never go back to your evil ways again, your sins may be wiped clean.

The law of nature should not be altered or tampered with for any reason. Nature must be allowed to take its course. When man alters nature from its given course, this often results in the uncomfortable tremor of nature attempting to return to its original course. This shaking often manifests in the form of natural disasters, pain, and sufferings. Our motivation should be to obey all laws — divine, natural, and man-made — to live blissful lives of well-being.

All laws are designed and enacted by God (the Creator of all things), with the exception of man-made laws, which are actually enacted, as the name implies, by man to establish an acceptable way to relate with one another. We will be attempting to explore each of the laws we mentioned above carefully in this chapter.

What Are Spiritual Laws?

Spiritual laws are divine laws that harmonize the relationship between God and man; as such, they are superior to all other laws. They are important because they govern how the entire universe functions and how the elements of creation interact. Considering the importance of spiritual laws, they should not be ignored but taken seriously. Think of them as the sky in which the birds fly.

To experience blessings and abundance, one must obey spiritual laws. It is ignorant for a man to walk contrary to spiritual laws, because many are not aware of the significance or importance of spiritual laws in relation to our existence.

Experiences are a school master that teaches a way of doing things better.

Some people have not yet become aware of the spiritual laws that govern mankind, while some have, but do not consider them to be of any importance. Some may never comprehend these laws, and, as a result, will consistently be in violation of them, thereby incurring grief while repelling divine favor and abundance. Nevertheless, any suffering you may have experienced today is intended not to punish you but rather to generate an awakening within that brings you to the desired conscious state of obedience.

Naturally, every man, at some stage of life, is ignorant of all laws. This is true with babies, who need the support and guidance of adults for all their physical and spiritual needs. It is an accepted fact: the only way to attain adequate knowledge and understanding of anything in life is through experiences. Life experiences that involve pain (which may arise from errors and ignorance) are often the purest form of knowledge acquisition. Experiences are a school master that teaches a way of doing things better. They help to unfold the mysteries of life, which may be necessary for the enlightenment of our soul. Through experience, the vail beclouding our vision and understanding of the natural and spiritual environment is lifted. Therefore, a man who was once guided will now become a guide to his offspring.

Natural Law

Natural laws fall into two basic categories. First, the laws necessary to uphold and harmonize natural objects. These laws, which are not influenced by man, are necessary if the world is to survive. They must function according to natural course. An attempt to alter these laws can be catastrophic. The law of gravity is a typical example of these laws.

> *Gravity is a force which tries to pull two objects toward each other. Anything has mass also has a gravitational pull. The more massive an object is, the stronger its gravitational pull is. Earth's gravity is what keeps you on the ground and what causes objects to fall. Gravity is what holds the planets in orbit around the Sun and what keeps the Moon in orbit around Earth. The closer you are to an object, the stronger its gravitational pull is. Gravity is what gives you weight. It is the force that pulls on all of the mass in your body.*
> **Source - Coolcosmos.ipac.caltech.edu**

Simply put, what goes up must come down. Gravity is the reason we do not float.

The force behind the law of gravity is referred to as gravitational force. Each law is backed by a force that enforces its functionality; one could also look at it as the power that executes the law. We can understand from this that a law without a force behind it will not function.

A second example of natural law is the law of reproduction. Every creature produces after its kind. Man gives birth to its kind, dog to dog, bird to bird, and so on. This order of reproduction must be respected. If the contrary happens, this is will be termed as freak of nature. For example, it is abnormal and against the laws of nature for man to give birth to dog or dog to cat. Such an occurrence would be inconsistent with the law of reproduction. However, man often does violate the law of reproduction by performing crossbreeds between animals of different species. Crossbreeding interferes with the perfect course of nature.

Rather than tampering with natural laws, man is to accept and adapt to what nature offers. It is man's duty to adapt to nature and his environment. This was true—and accepted—in times past, but in recent times, man has become preoccupied with efforts to adapt nature and his environment to meet his needs. In this way, man's actions are altering the laws that govern nature. Systematically and gradually, man is destroying the world. All catastrophes, from earthquakes to illnesses, result from man's foolishness and quest for civilization. Man's want is insatiable. The more we try to satisfy our needs, the more our need increases. As we recognize and acknowledge our inherent greed, we should learn to accept what nature has offered us, instead of trying to force nature to meet our needs.

Our fathers understood this principle and consequently respected nature. The modern man, however, has no respect for nature. We call the greed and selfishness that have become our way of living "industrialization." Meanwhile, our ozone layer has been eroded by pollution. Man's lifespan has been significant reduced due to the poor quality of air we breathe. With crime on the rise, the world is becoming unsafe to live in, all because man's wants increase with the desire to maintain social status and meet societal demand.

Man-Made Law

We will cover man-made law, the third type, briefly, because we are already used to it. These laws are classified into statutes, principles, and rules enacted to govern and bring to order the behavior of man through generally accepted societal norms. Some sort of "check" or force must be in place for people to obey man-made law. This law is enforced by the various courts of law, the government, and the police.

Interestingly, deviations from the three laws we discussed above can invoke one form of punishment or another. Sometimes, the punishment may be severe; violating the law of gravity may result in a severe fall, which can end in serious injury or even death. A violation of spiritual can be detrimental as well.

A Further Look at Spiritual Laws

Spiritual laws are superior to natural and man-made laws. Although they seem intangible since we cannot behold them with our naked eyes, they are more real than the remaining laws. These are divine laws made by the Creator of the universe, designed purposefully to govern every facet of man's existence. These laws govern the thoughts of our hearts, what we say and do, and our attitudes toward our fellow human beings, animals and nature.

This law can attract a very strong karmic or retributive effect that can be summed up in one statement: "Whatsoever thou soweth, that also shall you reap." You cannot sow corn and expect to reap an apple. Like begets like.

Spiritual law is pure and does not discriminate. It grants access to God's blessings and abundance.

Spiritual law is pure and does not discriminate. It grants access to God's blessings and abundance, success and peace, long life and prosperity. On the other hand, by violating spiritual laws, one denies oneself true blessings and abundance, invoking failure and blocking peace.

An understanding and obedience of spiritual laws is a must if you want to command true blessings and abundance. Those who are not mindful in obeying spiritual laws bring pain to their own souls. The fruits of disobedience are business failures, war, unrest, hunger, and famine, just to name but a few. All over the world today, there is civil unrest, war, genocide, famine, etc. This suggests widespread violation of the spiritual laws that would have us respect another man's property and honor his existence.

Is Spiritual Law Given to Punish Mankind?

Just as man-made laws are enacted to help align our behavior with one another's and help us conform to societal norms, spiritual laws are put into operation by the Creator to harmonize creation and existence and help man enjoy a life of bliss, blessings, and abundance. It is a misstatement to say that spiritual laws are meant to punish man. In fact, they are given to create a harmonious environment and bliss. Spiritual laws have both positive and negative sides — just like anything else. To drive this home, let's look at a physical example.

Water, clearly, is good. It quenches thirst, refreshes the body, and can replenish the soul when someone no more than looks at it. Yet improper use of water can be very fatal. Does that mean water is bad or harmful? No! Not at all — water is good. However, to enjoy water, we have to comply with certain principles that govern its use. Only once these principles are complied with do you maintain a balance that creates harmony between man and existence, and which supernaturally creates blessings and abundance.

Spiritual laws create a harmonious atmosphere beneficial to mankind, bringing the peace necessary for inner prosperity and outer riches. This is the true reason for spiritual laws.

Everything you enjoy in life today carries both benefits and danger. Electricity, for instance, provides us many advantages. It is used to generate power, which can be used to light, heat, refrigerate, and so on and so forth. In contrast, improper application of electricity can result in shock and death. The primary intention of the invention of electricity was not to electrocute or shock anybody. The inventor had one objective in mind: making life easier for mankind. We must learn to harness and use to our advantage the positive side of anything. This is the true meaning of life.

Everything Operates in Balance.

It takes both life and death for existence to maintain balance and stability. Someone must be born to life and someone also must die out of life for existence to be meaningful. A balanced body requires that man eat and excrete waste. To understand the true meaning of love, hatred must exist. It takes light (day) and darkness (night) to have a full day and allow us to appreciate both. It doesn't make sense to say you don't like night and wish for it never to come. Night must follow day if the complete circle of time is to be meaningful. This harmony is seen in the lifespans of day and night, which are approximately twelve hours each. Interestingly, both the day and the night understand their tenure and retire for one another when their time is up.

There is a saying that "too much of everything is bad." Put another way, a good life is one of balance—in every sense. For the maintenance of a balanced life, good rest must follow hard work; otherwise, the body system will break down. Work, work, work with little or no rest is harmful to your mental state. Too much rest and little or no work (exercise) also can instigate a detrimental effect on your physique and financial well-being.

Only after experiencing the state of lack can abundance emerge. Otherwise, it would be very difficult to define and identify abundance. It is through our understanding of war that we understand peace.

Every unpleasant state you may find yourself in suggests a violation of some form of spiritual law. For instance, if you start noticing lack, you are in breach of the law of giving and receiving. If you have formed the habit of receiving and not giving, you are creating a spiritual imbalance that will eventually cut you off from receiving; it is just a matter of time. The law of giving states that "what so ever a man soweth that also shall he reap." If you don't sow, you cannot reap. If you sow evil, you will also reap evil. If you don't give, you cannot expect to receive. This law is meant not to punish you but to draw your attention to areas in which you need to maintain balance.

Let me describe this principle with an illustration. Take a scale of measurement. "Giving" is written on one side and "receiving" on the other. If you have too much receiving on the scale and less giving, the scale will slant to one side, thereby causing imbalance. Every spiritual imbalance eventually creates an inharmonious reality around you. This reality can manifest in various forms, depending on the violation.

Be Quick to Identify Imbalances and Take Action to Correct Them

You are responsible for identifying where things are going wrong and taking steps to remedy these anomalies—and you must be quick to do so. Nobody will do that for you. This is your life; you must make the most of it now, both spiritually and physically. In the past, many were deceived by religious sects that proclaimed wealth is sinful. Some believe that riches are vanity. This is not true. There must be a balance between the natural and the spiritual for anyone to enjoy a life of bliss and comfort.

I agree that love for money is the root of evil, but this doesn't mean that you must not have it. Used to meet our needs here on earth, money is one of our most essential tools. But you must not seek it at the expense of your soul. I will be talking more about this later in chapter 5. Many are rich materially but have no peace or lack the understanding of the true meaning of life. (See chapter 3, "Why I'm Here").

As mentioned earlier, your obedience or disobedience of spiritual laws creates your physical or natural experiences. Most of today's rich nations suffer in terms of social disorders. For instance, America and Europe are classified as the richest regions in the world today, yet the governments of these nations have lost control and cannot enforce order because of their love for money. All their policies and decisions centered around money instead of morals.

Many books have been written on how to get rich quick, but nothing is said about the spiritual laws that govern all things, seen and unseen.

Human intelligence has substituted the laws of God. Anyone who believes that all the answers to his problems lie within him is being absurd; the answer to all problems is compliance with spiritual laws. We need to stop looking for so-called experts to solve our problems. Reliance on human intelligence is insufficient to solve the world's problems. The more man diverges from the spiritual laws and ways of God, the more catastrophes the world will experience. This is obvious now, as we see the world economic system has failed, billions of dollars are being wiped out in the stock market daily, sickness without cure is increasing, security systems have collapsed, poverty has reached its highest level ever, political unrest exists everywhere, and so on and so forth.

To endure, we must become, both individually and collectively, obedient to spiritual laws. Our present spiritual scale is imbalanced, tending to favor evil activities. There is an urgent need to start doing what is right by obeying spiritual laws, starting with respecting one another's right to exist.

Steps I Must Take to Balance Every Imbalance in My Life

1) I will commit to sit down every evening for at least fifteen minutes to review my activities and identify where I have hurt or cheated anyone, consciously or unconsciously. I will review my thoughts and relationships with others during the course of the day

2) I must be sincere in my analysis and repentant about anything that I have done wrong. This is true repentance.

3) I will sincerely commit to correct my wrongs the following day by apologizing to those I have offended

4) I will commit to respecting other people's views and be ready to share my opinion on matters with those who are involved

5) I will spend time seeking the truth about spiritual laws from the Holy Bible and be open for spiritual guidance.

2

Man: A Spiritual Being

Only a few are aware that they are spiritual beings. Many understand only their physical existence and fight anything that will challenge that understanding. Just like animals, many wake up in the morning and leave home to work for money, returning home late at night to sleep and then repeating the same thing again the following day. They live a vicious circle of survival all the days of their life, not knowing the true meaning of life.

I have heard many make the following statements: "Life's nothing," "Life is a game," "Life is meaningless," "Life has nothing to offer," "Life is hard," and so on. Such statements suggest that many are not aware of the real meaning of life. We are not here to experience grief in our souls.

An awareness of who you are will facilitate an awakening that will bring peace, abundance, and prosperity to your soul.

An awareness of who you are will facilitate an awakening that will bring peace, abundance, and prosperity to your soul.

You are a spirit. You have a soul that consists of mind and intellect, and you live in a body. In the truest sense, you are not what you actually think you are. This physical person that you claim to be will die one day, but the real you — the spirit — will live on.

Let's try to illustrate this with an example. When a man dies, you see him cease to function actively as every other man does. All his human attributes are still intact, but they are not operational. This obviously indicates that the spirit has departed. A body without the spirit is dead.

Since you are a spirit, you belong to the spirit world and are governed by spiritual laws.

Understanding this will help you refocus your attention to spiritual things, rather than the natural things we are given power to control. We truly have dominion over everything in this material world, but only a few know this truth.

Your Superiority over This Material World

You were created superior being over the natural world and its contents. Spiritual things are more real than physical things. As I mentioned earlier, what you do not see (the spirit) is more real than the things you see (physical). Inability to discern who you are will make it impossible for you to enjoy your true dignity.

What you place your attention on will ultimately dictate the reality you experience in life. The locus of your attention is very important. Devoting your attention and energy to the mundane things of this world will bring sorrow to your soul, but nothing in this world is more satisfying than the true love of God.

You must not become too attached to the things of this world, because there is no satisfaction in this. Rather, the attachment weighs down the soul.

Money, cars, fame, power, and political influence do not bring true satisfaction. If they do at all, this benefit is only temporary, and the satisfaction will fade with time. We have seen stars with great wealth and fame living a good life that anyone would desire. And, still, they look for peace and joy in drugs and alcohol. It is not surprising that some stars die from drug overdose; the world system is faulty. After attaining fame and great possessions, many realize that the peace they are looking for can't be found in possessions. Then they seek satisfaction elsewhere, in drugs and other harmful substances.

As technology has flourished, knowledge has increased. Economic experts and gurus coming up with fantastic monetary theories to combat the global economic problems the world is facing today, yet the world is getting deeper and deeper into serious recession. New technologies are being developed to help make the world a beautiful and peaceful place, but the world has only become more complex. Many books have been written on how to have a better marriage, yet the authors of those books battle with their own marriages. Seminars on how to get rich instantly are being organized daily, but the world is only getting poorer daily.

The solution for a world that has lost its grip can't be found in the world itself. It's about time we remove our confidence in man's ability to solve his problems and focus on the spiritual realm, where all solutions reside.

Man Has Lost His True Spiritual Identity

Too much focus is being placed on this physical world. Many place their confidence in man, hoping that the solution to their problem lies in the hands of experts. Meanwhile, we have completely lost the sense of who we are, where we came from, and where we are going. The majority believe that true life begins and ends here on earth. This is pure deceit and shows a complete loss of self-identity.

Before our society can experience peace and sanity, we need to look beyond this natural realm for help. I have heard many say the world has changed significantly, but I disagree. The world has not changed and will never change.

Everything, from day one, has remained the same. The sun rises every morning in the east and sets in the west every evening. The moon has its phases. Gravitational force, ordained from the beginning, has remained intact. This stability suggests that *the world* has not changed, but there are clearly differences. What, then, has changed? The answer is obvious: man! Let me prove this to you.

Many years ago, when people lived in small communities and were happy with what nature offered, there was peace. There was no murder and people lived long lives. The comfort the world offers has changed with time, simply because of a gradual shift from the being spiritual-minded to natural-minded beings.

The more we shift from spiritual-minded to natural-minded, the more catastrophes the world will experience.

The more we shift from spiritual-minded to natural-minded, the more catastrophes the world will experience. Sadly, even our leaders are pumping more resources into research on natural means of dealing with natural problems. This will not work; it is a complete waste of resources. Recommendations from this research will only multiply the world's burden. We need to focus on the unseen to solve seen problems.

Don't Get Too Attached

If you get too attached to this mundane world, you will lose focus on your true identity. Many hold on to unnecessary things at the expense of their soul.

I still vividly remember scenes from a cowboy film I watched years ago. In one, a group of thieves robbed the bank in this cowboy's city and escaped with several sacks of bills. The sheriff and his men gave chase. As the bank robbers made their way toward the desert, all except one were caught. The escapee made his getaway but ran into another group of robbers. When he saw them, he rode his horse faster to escape, but they chased him and shot at him several times. The sack of money the bank robber had tied to his horse tore, and the bills in the sack were blown all over the place.

The bank robber stopped and came down from his horse. As the bank robber gathered the bills together, he was shot in the back. As he bled profusely, obviously dying, this robber barely noticed the injury he'd sustained from the gunshot. He was too busy gathering the dollar bills blown around by the wind. Because of his injury and blood loss, he fell face-down and died on top of the few bills he'd managed to gather.

Several issues came to forefront from this story:

1. The guy traded his soul for the riches of the world.
2. He became too attached to this material world.
3. Money became more important to him than his soul.

Nothing in the whole world can buy anyone's soul. It is mere ignorance for a man to lose his soul for things that are pure vanity. The Bible says in Mark 8:36, "For what shall it profit a man, if he shall gain the whole world, and lose his own soul?"

People are too attached to this material world and the things in it. Many become enamored with money and the power associated with it at the expense of their souls. Everything in this world will perish, and an attachment to things that will eventually perish brings weariness to human soul.

The things of this world do not actually bring joy and comfort, as many have been made to believe. By the time people have accumulated the number of possessions they believe will make them happy, they realize that the promise of peace via material wealth is not true.

Anytime our focus is taken away from our true nature and the spiritual laws that govern all physical or material things, we burden our souls with unnecessary stress.

The most interesting thing about wealth is that those who have it want more, and those who haven't got it are looking for it. True happiness can found only in compliance with the laws of God. Be careful not to laden your soul with unnecessary burdens. True prosperity lies deep within. This concept is discussed in greater depth in a later chapter—prosperity starts from the soul.

Man is a spiritual being. Anytime our focus is taken away from our true nature and the spiritual laws that govern all physical or material things, we burden our souls with unnecessary stress. The symptoms of attachment to material things are usually stress and nervous breakdown. Do not spend time thinking of tomorrow, because tomorrow will take care of itself. This is a simple way to set your mind free from this world and its deceitful lost.

Money and material things are made for man, but man is not made for material things. Let go of all the worries and fears of the future. Take things one at a time. Everything you need to survive in this world has been provided for. To attract wealth and prosperity and live a life of peace and comfort, you must take your focus away from the natural circumstances surrounding you and begin to pay more attention to spiritual things. Admire nature. Walk by the sea, in a park, or through the woods. Observe flowers, plants, and the waves of the ocean; admire their beauty.

Wealth and prosperity will come to you naturally if you do not place your focus on them. Expending too much energy thinking of natural things blocks true prosperity. Instead, learn to redirect your thought energy on spiritual truth, because your natural reality takes its root from the spirit realm. If you can visualize the true love and abundance God has for mankind, you will experience wealth and peace in all facets of life.

Steps I Must Take to Attract Wealth and Peace

1) I must spend time praying for guidance and an understanding of the truth
2) I must confess these words aloud, once or twice daily, "I am a spiritual being, I possess the quality of God, and I am rich and wealthy. Abundance and peace are mine, and I claim them. My soul is free from the attachments of this world. Peace and comfort dwell within me."
3) I will not waste time thinking of my shortcomings. Instead, I will rather spend time thinking of love and peace.

3

The Thoughts of Your Heart

Thought is a force, or energy, that creates our reality. The most powerful spiritual tool a man has is the ability to think. Thought is a force, or energy, that creates our reality. Our thoughts can be classified into two categories: (1) positive and (2) negative. Thoughts are so powerful because they have the ability to influence our actions. Everything we do in life and every step we take corresponds to thought. Even our speech is influenced by our thoughts.

Since our thoughts are so powerful and create our reality, then the subject on thought must be taken serious. While everyone thinks, not everybody knows the great role thoughts play in our lives. Every fiber of our being is controlled by our thoughts.

Thoughts are expressed through spoken words. All our actions are direct products of our thoughts, and every success and failure in life stems therefrom. Thoughts are so powerful that our future hangs on them. Thought is a spiritual force or energy. Its abuse can be detrimental and can alter our destiny. Only by virtue of thoughts can man communicate with the spiritual realm. A negative thought brings about negative reality, while a positive thought brings about positive reality.

As a Man Thinks in His Heart

Thinking is part of life. We cannot be separated from the consequences of our thoughts.

Since we understand that our thoughts are a great, potent power that we possess, it is our responsibility to use them to enhance our destinies. Our thoughts have a very strong bearing on our life and the reality we are currently experiencing.

Thinking is part of life. We cannot be separated

from the consequences of our thoughts. Every decision related to anything, good or bad, is first conceived in the mind and then released in thought pulses that are thereafter followed by action.

To be prosperous and successful we must first be able to control our mind. The ability to focus our thoughts toward a constructive objective is very important. An idea starts in thought and is transformed into imagination; when it reaches the stage of action, we begin creating our reality. For instance, the thought of some evil happening to you will create fear that is capable of haunting you for a long time. Until that thought pattern is broken, this fear will maintain its stronghold. Likewise, thoughts of peace and affluence, when properly focused and channeled toward good actions, will create an atmosphere conducive for` prosperity.

Because thoughts are spiritual in nature, we are closely connected to those who think similarly to us. This connection is so powerful that our thoughts exert strong influence over our physical well-being. You can read the thoughts of people on their faces if you are sensitive enough.

Environmental Influence

Your environment and the circle of friends you mingle with can influence your thoughts positively or negatively. Culture is simply a thought pattern dictating ways of doing things that has been developed over time and been passed down from generation to generation in a given society, group, or ethnicity. Naturally, it is capable of molding individual thoughts.

If the culture of a people is wrong, that people's collective mindset will reflect the inadequacies contained in the culture, consequently affecting people's ways of doing things.

Culture is the greatest barrier to our thoughts. If the culture of a people is wrong, that people's collective mindset will reflect the inadequacies contained in the culture, consequently affecting people's ways of doing things. For instance, it is easy to identify an Englishman and an American. Though the English language is predominantly spoken by both sets of people, there are great cultural differences, and these differences affect the way each group thinks. Since immigrating to the UK twenty years ago from Africa, I have learned to think like an Englishman. It took me some time to fit into the English culture, because my mindset was completely different. I had to learn their ways, cuisine, and lifestyle before

I could adapt to their system.

Collective Thought Pattern

When a child is born into this world, he originally has his own mind and mindset, free from the world's influence, but gradually he develops and accepts societal norms as a way of thinking. If his society's culture is wrong, the child will grow up projecting mistaken thoughts. His outlook on life will be completely different from that of someone from another culture.

Collective thought patterns can exert great much influence on our thoughts and, as a result, create our reality — for better or for worse.

An average bushman from an African village will think and act differently than a New Yorker. The difference in thought does not make one superior or inferior; these differences are largely due to cultural influences existing in each society.

Collective thought patterns can exert great much influence on our thoughts and, as a result, create our reality — for better or for worse. Another factor that may influence our thoughts is our circle of friends. If spend time with friends who are drunkards and who do not see the need to become prosperous in life, we are in danger of being influenced to conform with the group norm and thereby ending up drunkards ourselves. On the other hand, if our friends are politicians, our thoughts and actions will be geared toward political achievement. This principle is the same in every aspect of life.

Children are open minded, and they learn from their environmental experiences. What we learn as children becomes habits we carry into adulthood. If these habits are positive, they will influence our thinking patterns positively and create a better future. Conversely, if the habits we pick up as we grow into adulthood are negative, they will affect our lifestyle negatively.

Parents need to understand the danger children in the wrong environment face. They came into this world not knowing the difference between good and evil, and they can learn these principles only from their environment. Parents are responsible for ensuring their children are taught to accept what is right and reject what is wrong in their surroundings.

Children, particularly during adolescence, suffer a great deal of peer pressure. During this time, they are influenced to try things detrimental to their well-being. They may want to try drugs, have sex, and so on. If they are not discouraged, poor habits are formed, their innocent thought patterns are altered, and correction can sometimes be very difficult as attempts to impose correction are strongly opposed.

Parents should remain observant by keeping tabs on who their children hang out with, the types of books they read, the movies the watch, and the kind of music they listen to. Corrupt mediums of entertainment can negatively influence children if not monitored.

We develop habitual thoughts through the use of our senses. This process usually occurs as a result of what we see (what we see and watch on television), what we hear (news and the kind of music we listen to), and what we feel. These are the three main activities that can influence and mold thought patterns in an individual over time.

What is a habitual thought? A positive or negative behavior developed as a result of environmental influence over a period of time, which has now become a way of living. Habitual thoughts come naturally, drawing unconscious conclusions from the physical or natural word. This type of thought pattern can oppose anything that is not natural, and it opposes things that are spiritual, because the natural and spiritual run parallel.

People who have developed habitual mindsets are not in control of their thoughts. Their minds draw conclusions from the natural word, and, as far as they are concerned, what they cannot see is not real. However, in a true sense, what is not seen is more real than what is seen.

Some people have progressed past this natural or physical realm and have developed the ability to control their thoughts. They spend time meditating daily on spiritual laws (i.e., the Holy Bible) and are quick to reject unpleasant thoughts that may creep into their mind.

The Mind Is a Battleground

All the issues of life take root in the mind. So many unseen forces fight to rule over a man's mind, because once the mind is captured, it can be easily influenced. The practice of mind control is very common among hypnotists. They manipulate the subconscious mind so their victims will conform to their requests. This is pure witchcraft and should be discouraged. Your mind belongs to you, and it is wrong for another person to put you into some form of trance and take over your mind and thoughts for any reason. Any infringement on your right to your thoughts is wrong.

I will reiterate here: everything we do starts with our thoughts. For instance, reading, eating, playing and talking must all first be thought of, and our thoughts will send signals to our body to take action.

We have the ability to generate positive thoughts or negative thoughts, and the thoughts we generate determine our experiences in

Every crime starts in thought form, taking suggestions from the environment. If such a thought is not quickly dismissed and replaced with a more positive one, it will develop into imagination, and, if not controlled, create your reality through your actions to fulfil your heart's desire. Just as negative thoughts bring about one's desire, so also do genuinely positive thoughts bring about positive results.

We have the ability to generate positive thoughts or negative thoughts, and the thoughts we generate determine our experiences in life. Genuine positive thoughts of peace and love toward mankind will creative a reality of peace and love for you. To enjoy good health, you must maintain positive thoughts of good health toward others. This fact is based on karmic law: "Knowing that whatsoever good thing any man doeth, the same shall he receive of the Lord, whether he be bond or free" (Ephesian 6:8).

To experience perpetual bliss, embrace this scriptural principle: "Whatsoever things are true, whatsoever things are honest, whatsoever things are just, whatsoever things are pure, whatsoever things are lovely, whatsoever things are of good report; if there be any virtue, and if there be any praise, think on these things" (Philippians 4:8).

Every Great Accomplishment Starts in the Mind

Success starts from the within. To experience true prosperity and success, a renewed mind is necessary. In one of my seminars, The Laws of Financial Empowerment, I told the students that our thoughts and our words held the same weight. They carry the same benefits, if applied positively, and penalties, if applied negatively, as the thoughts of our heart. The words we speak are our thoughts expressed vocally. As mentioned earlier, our thoughts are so powerful that they construct our reality.

With some people I have counseled, especially those worried about failing professionally even though their businesses were doing well financially, I have emphasized that they will fail only if they want to. The success or failure of most businesses is not a result of external factors, as many claim. No, failure is largely due to the fear of failure most business people have in their minds, as well as the negative factors they confess about their businesses. Even if external factors are involved, I strongly believe that they constitute only 20 percent responsibility, while 80 percent of the responsibility is traceable to fear and ill-spoken words over a period of time.

A man came to my office one afternoon about two years ago. He had started a grocery store somewhere in Deptford South East London about six months before, and since then, a lot of people had come into his shop but very few had purchased anything. The reason they didn't buy his wares was a mystery to him. He said he had checked to ensure his prices were comparable with those of similar area businesses, and he had determined that, for the most part, he was underselling his competitors. I decided to pay a visit to his shop to see if I could obtain any physical evidence for why he was not selling. To my surprise, the shop was on a busy high street in Deptford market, well lit, with items properly arranged/displayed and well-priced. Straightaway, I knew that his dilemma must have been largely spiritual rather than physical.

After an extensive counseling session, I found out that his marketing strategy was right, but his mindset was wrong. During the counseling, I noticed some vital issue that was mitigating his business.

1) From his very first day in business, he had maintained negative thoughts about the business failing and the shop closing

2) He had always confessed and expressed his fears through spoken words. Thoughts such as, "I am just waiting for the shop to close. The customers don't like me. I haven't got what it takes to run a successful business. I am not hoping to sell anything today because the customers don't buy anyway."

3) He carried a very strong ideation of business failure and supported this view with a strong imagination.

The first step I took was to teach him how to destroy the negative thoughts he had developed about himself and negative words he had spoken about the business, which were now forming a very strong reality against his business. After a three-month period of developing positive thoughts based on spiritual laws and forming positive affirmations about the business, it started to compete well.

The lesson we can learn from this story is that our successes and failures depend on how we see ourselves, not necessarily how others sees us. If we are to enjoy affluence and prosperity, we must obey the law of positive thinking and positive affirmation or confessions.

Learn to Focus Your Thoughts

"He that hath no rule over his own spirit is like

a city that is broken down, and without wall" (Proverbs 25:28). Improper application of our thoughts can prevent us healing physically as it weakens our defense system against sickness. Well-focused thoughts can bring about complete healing to our body and help us live a life of complete health.

... focusing on the pain and symptoms that arise from poor health can reinforce sickness and act as a barrier to healing.

Healing starts with the mind. Well-focused thoughts of scriptural laws about healing can bring total healing to our body. If we are to enjoy good health, we must begin by focusing our thought energy on good health. We must take our focus away from the symptoms, because focusing on the pain and symptoms that arise from poor health can reinforce sickness and act as a barrier to healing. Once you take your focus away from pain, you have begun the process of healing.

Sometimes, it can be very difficult to take your attention away from pain. This is true in most cases, especially if you have not effectively trained yourself concentrate and meditate on the laws of healing. The only way you can overcome this is by confessing scriptural words that promise you healing.

I remember well, sometime in November 2006, developing pneumonia; my lungs were heavy with sharp pains, I could not breathe properly, and movement was very difficult for me. I picked up my Bible and began meditating on scriptures of healing. I believed in the power of these scriptures, and I started employed my imagination to visualize my healing. Then I began confessing and proclaiming my healing aloud. I fought mightily to oppose anything that suggested I was sick, and, when I had created a focus capable of generating enough faith for my healing, I experienced a manifestation of healing in my body, and I was healed completely.

Acting on the word of God will generate the faith you need for your healing. That is exactly what I did.

Expand Your Mind

The most important aspect of enhancing your thought energy is expanding your mind. Our minds can only be expanded and function effectively if we educate ourselves. Reading and studying books and other people's writings is a very good way to expand our minds.

The most important aspect of enhancing your thought energy is expanding your mind. Our minds can only be expanded and function effectively if we educate ourselves.

Thoughts can only be as good as the mind carrying them. We need to renew our minds by studying and meditating, but we also need to be careful about the books we read, study, and meditate on. There is a computer language referred to as GIGO, which is an acronym that stands for "garbage in, garbage out." What you feed your mind dictates what your mind will produce as thoughts. As one example, when you habitually watch pornographic movies, you will eventually commit adultery or fornication. What you feed yourself is what your mind will ultimately produce in thought form, and what you will eventually form in reality.

Our mind is like a tract of fertile land. Whatever you plant on this land is what will grow, and at harvest you will certainly reap the fruit you planted. If you plant sweet grapes, at harvest you will reap sweet grapes. Likewise, if you plant bitter grapes, in due season, you will obviously reap bunches of bitter grapes. If you have a habit of dwelling on thoughts of murder and other crime, a corresponding vibe will be emitted and an evil energy will build up until it eventually creates a reality of crime or even murder.

We must see our mind as fertile ground ready to accept any seed planted, regardless of what kind of plant will be produced from that seed. This is exactly how our minds work. This is why you should avoid watching television if you can, and, if you need to, mind what you watch. Instead, spend time gaining spiritual knowledge.

Meditation is another good way to expand and exercise our minds. Meditate on the word of God daily, as this is an effective way to fortify our minds against the invasion of unwanted thoughts.

The best time to mediate is early in the morning. Wake up before everyone else to study and meditate. Spend at least one hour meditating on scripture every morning before leaving home. This act will renew your mind in addition to helping you guard against undesirable thoughts. In addition, you will be spiritually alert and sensitive.

Be Sensitive

We also need to be sensitive, physically and spiritually. Learning to be silent and think before talking will help. Be a man of few words, and ponder issues rather than talking without thinking. Write down any idea dropped into your heart. Also write down any dreams you remember, as this is a great way to connect with your subconscious. Your mind has a tendency to work while your body rests.

Every great invention began from a spark of thought. Be observant and learn to observe changes in your environment. Identify problems and then ponder how best to solve them.

The desires of your heart shall be granted. If you truly want to solve problems, you will receive the solution. This is a spiritual law. Every selfless desire shall be granted, so concern yourself with how to help others solve their problems.

In the same vein, every invention takes its root from need. The invention of the motor vehicle came out of the need to solve the problem of travelling miles on foot. From the dilemma of people hoping to communicate across countries, the telephone was invented.

Never shy away from problems, and neither allow profit to be your motive for doing good. Selfishness can act as a barrier to what is beneficial to mankind. There are great inventions advantageous to mankind in the spiritual realm that we have not yet tapped into, so beclouded have we been by selfish focus. If your motive for achievement is purely selfless, you will receive the spiritual empowerment necessary to accomplish your desire.

God knows what your needs are, and he joyfully make sure that those needs are met, thus permitting you to remove your own focus from your circumstances.

The traffic light was invented out of a desire to stop accidents. Let your desire to help mankind become a priority.

Why Am I Here?

Nothing happens by accident. All things in this world, animate and inanimate, serve a purpose. Carefully think about this. Some think that they are in this world by accident. A mistaken answer to the question of why we are here has caused misery in many individual lives and many realms of life — and science is no exception. Science claims that the universe emerged from some form of *big bang*, but this concept is grossly reliant upon physical facts, which always stand to oppose spiritual truth.

When physical facts are substituted for spiritual truth, people are often misled.

When physical facts are substituted for spiritual truth, people are often misled. There is so much suffering in the world today, precisely because many have trusted science and have come to believe they are in this world as the result of some mysterious accident. For this reason, a large proportion of the world's population are living carelessly and without consideration for spiritual laws.

I will underscore a truth mentioned at the top of this chapter: all things have purpose, and man is meant to harness them for his own benefit. Let's look at the example of trees: they provide oxygen, and man is constantly exchanging carbon dioxide for oxygen with the trees and plants. Trees also provide rest and shelter for birds, fruit for man, and wood that we can use to build our homes. These are just a few benefits we have derived from trees. The sun and the moon also serve a significant purpose for both mammals and plants. Rivers are a source of water supply needed by every living creature.

Man is not an exception. While man is superior, all of God's creatures have significant roles to play in the physical and spiritual development of mankind. Mankind's inability to understand this truth about his existence is what causes mayhem in the world today.

Man is blindfolded by greed and selfishness. It is absurd for a man to believe that life came from some kind of big bang, as science has purported. Look around you; you will agree with me that everything around us has a purpose and a role to play in this world. Man is no different.

God created everything in this world, including

man, and handed the world to man to tend to and look after. This earth belongs to us, and we are individually and collectively responsible for look after it. We must not allow our greed to destroy Mother Earth.

Since man has failed to comprehend the true meaning of life, our reason for being here has been substituted with greed and perverseness. The earth we are supposed to look after is being ruined by man's greed. Billions of pounds of toxic waste are being dumped into our oceans and emitted into the air.

This destruction could be stopped, but why does it continue? Because nobody is truly interested in saving the earth. Instead, we are concerned with satisfying our selfish aims. Wars all over the world, countries fighting against one another, widespread civil wars across African countries and the third-world countries rage on while Western countries—which have the power to halt the destruction—fold their arms and stand aside. This is sad.

Why do the superpowers do nothing about the problems in the world today? The simple answer is that they benefit from the global chaos. Some individuals are raking in billions of dollars from the sale of nuclear energy and arms to countries at war. That profit is what they care about, rather than the damage being done to the earth and the people being killed, the women widowed and children made fatherless.

Man has lost his true purpose. We have failed to realize that we are spiritual beings in human flesh. Selfishly we busy ourselves at the expense of our souls.

Man is responsible for the upkeep of this earth, for loving and looking after it with great care. We are not meant to tear it apart.

Everything Is Meant to Benefit Mankind

The mountains, the seas, the trees, the sun, the moon, even the animals were given by God for the benefit of mankind. What beauty do we behold as we walk in the woods, climb mountains, swim in rivers, bask in the sun, admire animals, listen to birds sing? An infinite beauty indeed.

Take a trip not to end up at a certain place, but to admire the journey—the nature around you. Learn to appreciate everything, and in return you will feel appreciated.

The joy we get from nature is priceless. I love nature; sometimes I sit on the couch in my front room simply looking at my garden and admiring the exquisite color of flowers in the sun. Sometimes, when it snows, the whole garden looks white. I sometimes walk in the woods to meditate and listen to songs from birds. What a beautiful way to relax and think things through.

I am granted much insight and inspiration when I admire nature. Just admiring nature reminds me of God's beauty and awesome power.

If nothing is done to preserve this beautiful world and its contents, we will end up losing it. Let's stand in defense of the earth. We cannot close our eyes and pretend that nothing is going wrong. The primary purpose of each and every one of us is to look after the earth with love. We must care for her. We must love her.

Love Your Neighbor as Yourself

As beautiful and gentle as love is, it is also powerful. Love is a spiritual principle that cuts across all aspects of life. God is love, and we are a part of a loving God. We ought to love everybody in this world. Love is so powerful that, properly applied it has the ability to tear down walls built in hatred and bring peace to mankind.

Love is the act of accepting people as we accept ourselves.

Love is the act of accepting people as we accept ourselves. Walking in love is selfless and is purely from the heart. Love will preserve you and bring love to you from others as you learn to walk in love.

For your love to be complete, you must first

love God, the source of all love, both spiritual and physical. Second, you must love your neighbor as yourself.

You must share your love, both spiritually and physically. When you determine that you will love anyone you come across, this is the spiritual aspect of love. Also, be ready to share what you have with others in need; this is the physical. Spiritual love is not complete. Love can be complete only when both spiritual and physical love are balanced. It is not sufficient to love in your heart and ignore the hungry. You cannot give thoughts of love and fail to care about those who are naked and need clothes. You cannot say you have love and neglect those who are sick or in need of shelter.

If you have true love in your heart, and if that love is truly genuine, it will generate a burden in you to physically share others' pain.

Don't deceive yourself; true love is selfless. The acid test to determine if you love is when you are burdened in your stand against injustice and oppression. Second, sincerely share what you have with others and give joy to others.

True love does not seek a reward. Anything you do with the strong desire to profit from is not love; it is greed by a more noble name.

Pray for those suffering whom you cannot help or reach physically. Tell people sweet and kind words that will give them joy. For example, tell people you come across, "You are beautiful," and "I love you," and so on. When you improve someone's day and mood in this way, they may go home and spread the positive energy.

Be quick to share in the pains of those in grief, and be quick to pray for areas that have experienced natural calamities, such as earthquakes, tornadoes, and floods, and donate what money you can toward relief aid, thus helping return the lives of victims to normal.

Only when your love is complete can you enjoy the abundance of God through peace, finance abundance, and abundance and prosperity in your soul.

Steps I Must Take to Enjoy Abundance in Life

1) On a regular basis, I must check what I am thinking. I will do all I can to make sure I think only loving and pure thoughts.

2) Thought is a creative force. I will seek to control my thoughts by thinking exclusively about that which is pure, loving, and peaceful.

3) I will break away from cultural thinking by studying and meditating on the word of God.

4) I will spend at least ten minutes a day praying for the peace of the world.

5) I will not engage in actions that will destroy the earth, even if they are profitable.

6) I will wish love for everyone I come in contact with. I must also speak words that are edifying to everyone around me.

7) Every evening before going to bed, I will spend a few minutes emptying myself of the negative thoughts I have imbibed during the course of the day. I will sit down in an armchair (preferably), close my eyes, and review my thoughts from that day. I will identify negative thoughts and ask God to empower me to overcome them on a daily basis.

8) I will make this confession: I have the mind of Christ. I have the mind behind creation.

9) My thoughts are pure; my thoughts are noble and creative. I think of only those things that are pleasing to God, because I have the nature of God. I can identify problems and I desire to solve the problems of the world. I love God, I love my neighbor. Love releases the abundance and prosperity of God into my life. Amen.

4

Give and Receive

We are a part of a universe of giving and receiving. Therefore, it is a law that we must give if we are to receive.

Here is another powerful law of abundance that cannot be ignored or despised: giving engenders receiving. Anything that is worth receiving is also worth giving.

God Almighty has

given and gives to us endlessly, and he expects to receive thanks. When we give thanks and appreciation to God, he in turn showers us with his love and abundance.

We are a part of a universe of giving and receiving. Therefore, it is a law that we must give if we are to receive. Giving should be a lifestyle. Frame giving in your thoughts not as a favor to the recipient but as an opportunity to be blessed.

Giving Is Sowing

Harvest succeeds sowing. To reap, you first must plant. Everything we do in life, whether good or bad, is sowing, and we — naturally, in due season, and in the same measure as our efforts — reap what we have sown.

Giving has a karmic effect on the giver. "For whatsoever a man soweth, that shall he also reap" (Galatians 6:7). Whatever you sow is what you will reap, but in good measure, pressed down, shaken together, and run over. We must be mindful of what we sow, because sowing does not have to be material; it can also be spiritual. When we wish others evil in our hearts, we have also sown a seed. Remember, every seed sown into good ground will bring forth a plant and eventually yield fruit after its kind. This is the law.

Let me explain this aspect of planting with an example. A seed bearing bitter fruit, when planted, will with time produce a plant yielding bitter fruits. Likewise, a seed yielding sweet fruits will also produce sweet fruits after its kind over a certain time. You may have noticed that I used the word seed (singular) and the word fruits (as plural). A single seed gives birth to a plant, and the plant will yield fruit, sometimes thirty-fold, sixty-fold, or even hundred-fold.

I remember well from my growing up how we would plant seeds on our ample land, ranging from creeping plants (like melon and ground nuts) to seeds of trees (like mango). So, I know very well what sowing and reaping mean.

We don't sow a seed of corn and expect to reap banana. Interestingly enough, the banana has a bit of religious significance, according to Ray Comfort and Kirk Cameron.

Ray Comfort, also known as "Banana Man," made a strange argument about bananas. He considered the banana's ease of use, nutritional value, and "color-coding" to be irrefutable proof of intelligent design. The banana is, after all, curved toward the face for ease of consumption and does not squirt in one's face when bitten into.

Likewise, a singular good deed has the ability to spiritually and physically replicate itself in multiple fruits on harvest day.

Give What You Desire Most

Understanding how to give is very important. Just as a seed must be sown in fertile ground to yield its increase unto us, we need to know how and what to give.

...the best thing to give is what you desire most. If you desire to be loved, begin giving love.

There is no limit to what we can give or what we should give. Our giving can be spiritual in the form of prayer. Simply saying a short prayer for a person, a family, or a nation can go a long way. It is the same with hoping someone who is sick becomes well.

Giving can also be material, for instance, giving money, food, clothes, shelter, and more.

But the best thing to give is what you desire most. If you desire to be loved, begin giving love. If you are a Christian and what you desire is money, start giving money in the form of tithes and offerings. Give to charities and other good causes as well.

I would like to emphasize money, because money is a vital life force and an important subject in today's world. I must warn here that we must not love money, because, as the popular aphorism goes, money is the root of all evil. We can desire to have it, as it will solve most of our material problems, but we should never love it.

We need money to provide our basic needs, ranging from shelter and clothing to food, but this does not require that we become attached to it. Always remember that, although money can buy you a big house, it cannot buy you a home. You can buy good clothes but not health, good food but not an appetite. Money is not worth dying for.

When you give good things, you attract good things to yourself. Likewise, by giving money, you create an environment conducive to receiving money in good measure. This is a spiritual law.

If you want to experience financial abundance, give monetarily. Obey spiritual commands by regularly and honestly paying your tithe, which is 10 percent of all your earnings. Also, obey physical demands by giving to everyone who asks of you. Give to the poor and donate to charitable causes.

You may say, "But I don't have enough to give." Start by giving from the little you have. The amount doesn't have to be big, but by starting now, you can experience abundance in the area of your finances. Start reaching out to your fellow man by giving money to those you sincerely know need to satisfy their basic needs.

Secret Giving Is Powerful

Know this: any giving not done secretly is incapable of releasing financial increase. Only secret giving, the kind that seeks no publicity, can yield abundance for the giver.

The Lord Jesus Christ warned sternly: "Take heed that ye do not your alms before men, to be seen of them: otherwise ye have no reward of your Father which is in heaven" (Matthew 6:1).

He made it clear that the only giving capable of generating receiving is done privately: "When thou doest thine alms, do not sound a trumpet before thee, as the hypocrites do in the synagogues and in the streets, that they may have glory of men. Verily I say unto you, they have their reward" (Matthew 6:2).

This principle of giving secretly is so important that even close friends shouldn't know about it. "But when thou doest alms, let not thy left hand know what thy right hand doeth" (Matthew 6:3).

Jesus knew the potent power contained in secret giving. Secret giving engenders receipt of abundance. "That thine alms may be in secret: and thy Father which seeth in secret himself shall reward thee openly" (Matthew 6:4).

Give More, Receive More

Giving has a strong magnetic force invisible to the physical human eye that attracts receiving to the giving soul.

The more you give, the more you will receive. Giving consistently will make you a perpetual receiver. I know of a man who gave more than 40 percent of his wealth to a charity. A few years later, he became richer than he had ever been.

Giving and receiving must operate based on love. A need must be identified or perceived, and action to meet that need must then be initiated through giving. That giving must in turn be capable of generating satisfaction for the receiver, for the law of giving and receiving to be effective. Any giving that does not satisfy a need is not giving, and no receiving will follow.

For example, if you know that someone needs school fees and you have more than enough to pay but instead you give him some lousy amount of money not even sufficient to buy a meal, you are fully aware that your gift will not solve his problem. This type of giving does not meet a need and will therefore generate no money received.

Any giving that produces receiving must meet a need and be capable of generating joy to both the giver and the recipient.

It's important to acknowledge at this juncture that sometimes you may not have enough to meet a need for someone, but you may want to contribute toward meeting that need to the best of your ability. This type of giving is very effective, because it shows concern and love. While lousy giving will not be rewarded, this type of giving will be.

What do I mean by lousy giving? This type of

giving is giving that fails to come from the heart. It is a giving motivated by selfishness, with no true meaning or purpose. Because it has no spiritual force behind it, it will amount to nothing.

Do Not Doubt

A fearful or doubting spirit is a very dangerous one. This spirit has hindered many from experiencing fulfillment in life. Fear builds an invisible wall that, if not destroyed immediately, acts as an obstacle to abundance and blessings.

Someone once defined fear as *"force evidence appearing real,"* and I agree with this definition. Fear is not real, but if it is conceived in the mind for a long time, it will eventually metamorphose from spiritual to physical. In other words, it will become real.

Fear is a strong spiritual force that must be dealt with when noticed before it takes root.

Fear is a strong spiritual force that must be dealt with when noticed before it takes root. In this way, fear is simply a habit. Any habit not counteracted will eventually solidify into a stronghold.

Any giving done in fear or in doubt has no spiritual energy behind it and, therefore, will not trigger the receipt of gifts or abundance. For giving to generate receiving, faith is a necessity.

Faith is the bridge between giving and receiving. Fear and faith cannot coexist; you are either fearful or you have faith.

Faith is the supernatural force that translates giving into receiving, and you must believe this to benefit from it. (See chapter 8 for more on the topic.)

Sacrificial Giving

Rooted in love, sacrificial giving is the highest form of charity; all other types are secondary. Sacrificial giving is additionally the purest form, cutting across the walls of selfishness with a loving state.

This type of giving is practiced when you forgo a benefit owed to you for the sake of another person, when you give up what you have rightfully harvested to relieve someone else's need. This powerful incarnation of giving produces abundant receiving.

Sacrificial giving can come in several forms, but I will give few examples here.

1) When you pray for others to relieve their pain, even though you too are going through pain
2) When you offer your food to another person who is hungry, when in fact you yourself

are hungry

3) When you give up an important commitment to save a life. Take the example of a man who saved every cent he could lay his hands on for a number of years to pay for holiday for his family and himself. The children have told their friends at school and their neighbors that they are going on a vacation, and everybody, including his wife, is anxiously awaiting the holiday. Then one evening, Daddy comes in looking tired with unpleasant news to tell the family. Children and wife sit around him, patiently waiting to hear what he has to say. Then, the man slowing mutters with a soft voice, "We are not going on this holiday anymore. We are postponing our holiday to next year." Everybody is astonished by this news, and the children burst out, "Why, Daddy?" He scratches his head carefully, looking for words to explain his decision. He lifts up his head, looks at the children, and says, "Someone else needs the money for the holiday more than us. We were going on holiday for pleasure, but there is someone who needs a heart bypass operation to save his life but doesn't have enough money. I think it will be a better thing for us to miss this holiday and save a

life than to go on holiday and allow someone to die."

This is a big sacrifice, isn't it? Sacrificial giving of this nature, that comes at such a high cost, has the potent energy to engender receiving in an incredible propensity.

What an astounding way to give. You can see that this type of giving is motivated solely by love, and anything done in love is not selfish but selfless.

> *Selfishness builds a wall or barrier that continues fortifying itself spiritually and, over time, becomes a stronghold that repels receiving.*

Selfishness builds a wall or barrier that continues fortifying itself spiritually and, over time, becomes a stronghold that repels receiving. As an old adage says, you can't have your cake and eat it too. Selfishness and greed act as acid, corroding your finances and thwarting your opportunity to be blessed. Selfishness is like a virus that eats up good cells in the human body if not treated. We must help in doing God's duty to give, selflessly, to those in need. He bled for us; we must bleed for him. If you want to experience abundance and prosperity, you must do away with all forms of selfishness and become a giver. A familiar biblical saying proposes that givers never lack, and this is true. As you begin to give out of love, you pave the way for abundance and prosperity into your life.

Dead Giving

Any giving that is dead has no life and will not yield anything. And whatever it may possibly yield will be equally lifeless—incapable of producing good or gain.

Based on the law of reproduction, everything produces after its kind (see chapter 6). And just as animals produce only the young of their own species, death will produce death and life will reproduce life.

Only giving that contains life is capable of generating receiving that contains life as well. And the only thing that will inject life into your giving is love, which is the life force behind every gift.

I always consider an opportunity to give an opportunity to be blessed. When I started writing about giving and receiving, a man came to my office and asked reception if he could see someone who could help him. I believe the receptionist misunderstood him. She called my office and told me there was someone from Holland at the reception asking to see me concerning some church issues. I asked her to send him in, and, within seconds, a man in his late fifties and a young guy walked into my office. Apparently, they were father and son. They told me they were missionaries travelling around Europe and asked for money to buy fuel and food. Without hesitation, I gave them enough for what they needed. The next day, another man came to my office asking if he could swap his benefit check for cash. On the evening of the third day, I pulled into a supermarket parking lot with my wife and daughter to get some money out of the ATM. A man approached me to ask for some money for food. I gave each of these people something that was somehow sufficient to give them food. I did this in love because I personally hate to see anyone go hungry. This is the kind of passion that has the ability to replicate abundance for the giver.

You Are Part of a Giving Order

Giving and receiving keep the universe in perfect motion. We cannot opt out of the unique order established by this law.

Giving and receiving is a law, and a very powerful one. Many do not yet understand this concept, and even among those who do, many have not released the potential to receive. Both comprehension of the idea and practical application are needed to bring abundance. I have heard many talk about giving and receiving, displaying a clear understanding that the former is good, but few practice this unique principle God has deliberately put in motion to bless us.

Giving and receiving keep the universe in perfect motion. We cannot opt out of the unique order established by this law. By attempting to break this order, we exclude ourselves from its potential benefits.

We should strive to partake in this unique order, and enjoy the abundance God intended for us, by becoming committed givers. Let me reemphasize: when we give, we are bound to receive. This is the law.

Giving Is Profitable

Please do not think that your giving will go unnoticed, or that you will receive nothing in return.

When you give with love, some form of unexplainable joy and peace permeates your entire being.

It is true that giving is profitable, and our ability to balance the law of giving and receiving is what makes this law profitable. There is a need to balance giving and receiving. We must not be on the receiving end all the time without balancing the scale through giving.

This law works in two ways. When you give, you receive, and when you don't give, you don't receive. It is more blessed to give than to receive.

Apart from the gifts you receive in return, giving offers the benefit of peace to your soul. When you give with love, some form of unexplainable joy and peace permeates your entire being. A group of friends and I take food and clothing to the homeless once in a while. Anytime we do this, we share in the joy that we bring them. For days and weeks after, I feel very joyous and peaceful within.

For any giving to be profitable, it must first be selfless and done out of pure love. Any giving orchestrated out of selfishness, to attract favor from another person, will not engender receiving. Such giving lacks the energy to generate receiving because it is embellished with self-centered desires.

Receiving Can Come in the Form of a Concept

After receiving will follow giving, it may not necessary appear similar to what you gave. Some people believe that after giving they can sit back and wait for someone to knock on their door with sacks of gold coins laden on the back of a camel, saying, "I am an angel sent by God to deliver these gold coins to this address." No! It doesn't work that way.

If you haven't yet consistently kept the law of giving and receiving, there are certain steps that you must take to experience abundance. Don't just give and go to bed, doing nothing more and expecting a miracle. This attitude will lead to slavery and penury.

I am not saying that when you give, people won't bless you in return. Usually—maybe 80 percent of the time—heaven will reward you with an idea or a concept capable of generating abundance and wealth. What you do with this concept is entirely up to you.

Heaven is constantly giving back spiritually to givers in the form of concepts and ideas. Since you are both a spiritual and physical person, you have the ability to operate in both capacities, communicating with God even as you complete your natural assignment.

Once you position yourself to receive from God through your giving, heaven will begin to throw rich ideas and concepts at you.

You are a bridge between the spirit and the physical world. You receive from the spirit and translate what you received from the spirit to the physical world.

The Relationship between the Spirit World and the Physical

World

Everything seen in the physical world is rooted in the spirit world. Whatever we experience here on earth has first been conceived in that spiritual realm.

Once you position yourself to receive from God through your giving, heaven will begin to throw rich ideas and concepts at you. As a giver, you must be sensitive to these spiritual things. When you indulge regularly in prayer, your spiritual self becomes sensitive to the Spirit of God.

Through your acceptance of the fact that God is the source of all wisdom, you will enhance your access to that same wisdom.

Don't throw your ideas or concepts away. They are given by God to reward you for your giving. God expects you to receive from Him and translate his gift into the material world. If you don't know how to go about translating your idea or concept from thought form in your mind, then ask for wisdom through prayer. Angels will be sent to empower you and assist you from the concept stage through the idea's physical manifestation. Isn't it wonderful to know we can receive angelic assistance to help us translate our vision into reality?

Don't bin or trash a concept. Doing so could be very costly. Every invention, great or small, started as a concept. Imagine if the idea to invent an airplane had not been acted upon by a pair of visionaries. We might still be travelling on seas for weeks or even months to arrive at our destination. This is true of all inventions.

As a giver, you have greater access than a nongiver to the rich ideas from heaven. Please don't waste this blessing. Don't cast your pearls before swine. They are too precious to be ignored. Your success and financial breakthrough is embedded in that concept you are conceiving right now, so give that concept the wings to fly high. You can do it. Remember that your thoughts create your reality. Do not be afraid take a bold step. Bear in mind that every great success starts from a concept, vision or idea.

Put Your Concept to Work

The best way to receive is usually in the form of rich concepts and ideas. I used the word *rich* because the ideas heaven throws at you are sourced directly from the rich mind of God.

Concepts and ideas are the mind of God revealed to mankind. This is great! But, as a result, it is an abomination to waste or do nothing with them. Quite a number of givers still struggle financially because they have not been correctly taught how to receive. They usually expect some kind of miracle that requires no action on their part. Please make no mistake: it is up to you to translate your concepts from thought to reality; some form of input will be needed from you.

What you say is very crucial to your success in life (See chapter 7 on affirmation). Confess daily that you have the ability to achieve what has been set forth for you. Pray for guidance and wisdom to accomplish your objective, and begin acting on your concepts and ideas. If you don't do anything yourself, nobody will, and you will receive nothing.

Steps I Must Take to Activate the Law of Giving and Receiving

1) I will always remind myself that I belong to a universe that is consistently giving and receiving.
2) I will be conscious of my relationships with those around me and what I do to others, because I am responsible for my actions.
3) I will give money to charitable causes and the poor.
4) I will be ready to forgo my pleasure to save life.
5) I will give and expect to receive without doubting the power of giving and receiving.
6) I will remain open to receiving concepts and ideas from God.
7) I will meditate on this confession: I have given, and it has been given unto me in good measure, pressed down, shaken together, and run over.

5

Prosperity Starts in the Soul

Your mentality dictates your desires in life, and you can never attain what you do not believe in.

To prosper in life, you must ensure your soul plays a significant role. For you to eventually find wealth and abundance in the natural realm, you must begin by conceiving prosperity at the soul level.

A prosperous mentality is crucial to experiencing abundance. Your mentality dictates your desires in life, and you can never attain what you do not believe in. If your mind is not prepared for wealth, you may accumulate some by accident but you will eventually lose it; it takes the right mindset to sustain money you receive.

If you hold a negative mentality about wealth and abundance, if you do not believe in success in life, then failure is inevitable. Remember, a strong desire maintained over a period of time will attract thoughts of its kind and eventually create your reality (see chapter 6).

Just as success is a desire come true, failure is a different desire come true. Interestingly, successful people will tell you success has always been their dream while those who've failed will tell you that they never wanted to fail—but neither did they specifically want to succeed.

I vividly remember an interview with a football team who'd won their entire tournament. The secret for this success was their desire, belief, and dream to win all their tournaments that season. They said, "We were focused, in good shape and worked hard and just believed that nothing is going to stop us from winning the tournament." The captain of the group said, "It has always been my dream to win this tournament. I desired it more than anyone else, because I know that winning will make a lot of difference to my life." And they won.

Let's look at another scenario: a very good basketball team that, one season, did very poorly.

They were the bookies' favorite to win the tournament that season, yet they lost every game they played. Their argument was, "We were not in form this time around. Things just didn't start well for us this season. There was no unity amongst us. We just knew that we weren't going to do well this season." And, indeed, they didn't do well. What a disappointment to the bookies.

What others think about you doesn't really matter; what you think about yourself does. If friends and family can count on you to succeed because they know you are talented or brilliant, that only matters to a certain extent. It's true that what others think of you can encourage and motivate you, but what you think about yourself supersedes the belief of others.

Take the example of the basketball team above. The bookies, the fans, and essentially everybody else believed they would win the tournament, but the team's belief contradicted the general confidence others had in them. On the other hand, we've all seen situations in which people didn't have confidence in a certain team or individual who, nonetheless, came out a winner—because they believed in themselves.

God created Mother Earth and embedded it with resources and wealth. It is your responsibility to discover it. I don't personally believe that resources are scarce; the insistence that they are is born of ignorance. Let me explain what I mean. We are called to discover wealth and harness it for our advantage. Everything around us is potential wealth. Unless you understand this concept, you may never discover the wealth nature has to offer you. Everything around us has the capacity to generate prosperity. To some, the sand we walk on, the cans we throw away, and our food waste is latent profit. Yet, as far as others are concerned, this material is rubbish and good for nothing.

Even the grass from your garden that you cut and throw away can generate income when used as animal feed. The skins from animals are used for leather. Sunlight, apart from generating light and vitamin E, generates solar energy to power electricity; wind is also used to spin turbines for the collection of electricity. From these few examples, you will appreciate that wealth is all around us. It is sheer ignorance that leads to the belief that resources are scarce.

To enjoy the wealth and abundance around us, we must cooperate with nature and align ourselves positively with its flow, rather than cutting ourselves off from its abundance.

The spirit dictates all happenings in this physical realm. Our thoughts have a very strong link with the spirit and forms what we say. Jesus said in Luke 6:45 "…For out of the abundance of the heart his mouth speaks".

Thoughts and what we say are spirits and have a very powerful ability to create our reality. When we believe in wealth and abundance and talk about it positively, spiritually, we create an atmosphere conducive to harmonious connection to the flow of wealth and abundance. On the other hand, when we believe in lack and talk about it regularly, it is only a matter of time before lack shows up on our doorstep.

I heard the story of a certain homeless man. I don't know how he became homeless, but he had a positive mentality directed toward success. While in the homeless hostel, he told all his mates that he would come out of the hostel a millionaire. His consistent boasting irritated his colleagues as nothing about him suggested he would ever be rich, much less a millionaire. Over time, everybody in the hostel started making jokes about him, calling him "poor millionaire." Yet he was not deterred by the jesting of his colleagues. His belief and confession remained constant. And his belief created his reality. A few years later he left the sheltered accommodation a millionaire, just as he had envisioned.

I'll share with you another quick story involving positive thinking. This one demonstrates how we have a choice, always, when it comes to how our day will go.

I was at the beach with friends once, in what

was to be only a day trip. Instead of dreading my return home that night, I pictured myself spending the night at the beach. I would get a room somewhere, somehow, and enjoy the holy sunrise the next morning as it lit the midnight-blue beach in gleaming silver.

My friends and I were out to lunch at the beach when along came a waiter my friend happened to know from high school. The waiter had a house on the beach and invited us to stay for the night! So you see, all my positive thinking had paid off!

Dreams and Visions

Dreams and visions help us generate and maintain focused thoughts, regardless of adverse

Dreaming help us to stabilize our thoughts and maintain our beliefs about our desired objective. When we see our future desire in dreams and visions through visualization or imagination, our attitude toward achieving those desired objectives becomes more aggressive. Naturally, we can much more easily believe what we have seen than what we have not seen.

Dreams and visions help us generate and

maintain focused thoughts, regardless of adverse circumstances. Martin Luther King, the civil rights activist who fought for the equal rights of Afro-Americans, famously said, "I have a dream." Despite facing great obstacles in his fight for the freedom of his people, he remained focused because of his dream. Though he lost his life in this fight, his dream lived on and became a reality. Dreaming is a powerful tool in the school of success, so powerful that it can outlive the dreamer.

If you can dream it, you can have it. But, whatever you cannot dream, you cannot have.

Dare to Take Risks

Risk is what I would refer to as acting in faith. To experience wealth and abundance, change is necessary. A shift from the left to the right is the first step of faith. When Peter complained that they had toiled all night and caught nothing, Jesus instructed him to launch into deep water. Although hesitant initially, Peter did as he was told and experienced abundance.

Positive thinking is good, but, more importantly, you must be determined to take the first step toward a new direction. You must be prepared to step out of your old ways. Many people are in bondage and lack today, because they are too comfortable and afraid of taking the risk to break out of their usual routine no matter how unfruitful it is. They are afraid of change and challenges.

Fear Converts to Bondage

Your mind needs to be completely free from unnecessary cares that have beclouded your rich ability to reason and think positively.

Many are in bondage today because they fear losing their comfort—they worry about what they will eat, what they will wear, whether they will fall sick, and so on. As a result, they have altered their thoughts negatively. Their concern is centered on working for a monthly salary to pay bills at the end of the month. This is a vicious circle many find themselves in. Any slight shift in their spending pattern is met by borrowing. For this reason, many are also in serious debt. They work simply to meet immediate obligations and, as a result, have become slaves to their employers since they cannot afford to lose their jobs. Under these conditions, it has become very difficult for many to take substantial but rewarding risk.

To experience wealth and abundance, you need to free your mind from any unnecessary weight. Not until you are free from fear and worry will you be able to put the positive and creative aspects of your mind to work. Remember that your thoughts create your reality. As long as you remain in fear of meeting monthly expenses, the possibility of getting out of this cycle is very slim.

Renew your mind by praying and reading the scriptures. Jesus said that you should take no thoughts for tomorrow. One of the songs in *The Jungle Book* states you should forget about your worries and your strife. Your mind needs to be completely free from unnecessary cares that have beclouded your rich ability to reason and think positively.

Be Still

Through prayer, we are able to achieve a level of stillness cable of breaking down the external forces that invade our minds with fears, worries, anxiety, and emotions.

"Be still and know that I am God" (Psalm 46:10). To reach the inner depth of wisdom within your soul, where lies the true source of wealth and abundance, you must be still. Turbulence will make your vision blurry, but stillness will enhance the quality of your foresight.

Stillness can only be attained through silence. Silence, in turn, is possible only if we withdraw from the noise around us once in a while to pray and meditate in spite of our busy schedule.

Through prayer, we are able to achieve a level of stillness cable of breaking down the external forces that invade our minds with fears, worries, anxiety, and emotions. Only then we are able to reach into the richness of our spirit and commune with the spirit of God, which is the source of pure wisdom, abundance, and wealth.

Our five senses present a serious obstacle to our spiritual advancement. We must be able to transcend the realm of our senses into the realm of the spirit, or what I will call the realm of God. In this elevated sphere of truth, there is no discrimination. It is a realm where all things are pure and beautiful, where the mind of God is revealed to mankind concerning any issue. This realm can only be achieved through prayer.

True wealth and abundance lie within. Regular prayer and meditation will make them blossom.

Steps I Must Take to Harness the True Prosperity within Me

1) I must believe that I possess all it takes to succeed.
2) Prosperity lies deep within my soul. I must reach it.
3) Every day, in the evening before going to bed, I must spend some time in silent prayer.
4) I must be alert and reach within for true wisdom through prayer, studying the scriptures and meditating on the word of God.
5) I must have a clear, definite objective in mind. Vague objectives cannot command success. I must know and be convinced of what my goals are.
6) I must have a strong desire to succeed and allow the desire to dominate my thinking process every day until a strong desire arises in me.
7) I must visualize my desired objective and possible outcome. I must see myself enjoying it.
8) I must stop complaining.

6

The Law of Attraction

This is another powerful law I cannot afford not mention in this book. I refer to this law as the law of magnetism, because it works just the same way a magnet works. A magnet contains a powerful force that attracts another piece of metal to it. I remember when we were small we used to play with magnets, but we realized they wouldn't pull aluminum and other items that were not metal.

There is an old saying that birds of same feather flock together. In the same way, you attract people with thoughts similar to your own. For example, it is a lot easier for someone in the same profession to make friends with those in the same profession.

A drunkard will usually make friends with fellow drunkards. Drug dealers will pair with other drug dealer, junkie with junkies, and so on.

This is because like attracts like. Having this understanding, if you want to have important, valuable friends, you must change your thinking. Thoughts are very powerful form of spiritual energy, and, just like magnets, they pull or attract to you people who form the same thoughts as you.

Your thoughts play a great role in your ability to live a prosperous life and enjoy divine health.

Your thoughts play a great role in your ability to live a prosperous life and enjoy divine health. If you dwell on thoughts of poverty and sickness, you will eventually attract these negative qualities. A concentrated thought of healing will eventually generate good health.

To enjoy good and abundance in life, you have to train yourself to think accordingly. A man who cannot control his thoughts is like a city without walls. Recognizing that you attract what you think of, remain conscious of what you allow in your mind.

To attract love, develop the habit of thinking of only those things that are loving. Send thoughts of love to others. Likewise, when you wish others to get well, you attract divine health.

Apart from your thoughts, your deeds are also crucial. To attract abundance and wealth, you must be committed to helping others have abundance and wealth. Help others get rich. If you have valuable information that others could benefit from, don't hide it. Share it with others. Commonly, people hide information that others will benefit from. I am not saying you should give your business secret away, but what I am trying to explain here is that you should share information that others can financially benefit from. For example, if you have some techniques on how to profit from trading share, share them with others.

Empower Others

This is another power that attracts wealth and abundance: teach others how to succeed. Don't hide anything that others could benefit from. If you do, you are creating a barrier to your own abundance and wealth.

As you continue to empower others to fulfil their destinies, you attract invisible helpers (Angels) to yourself.

When you share with others information vital to their success and wellness, you create an atmosphere conducive to receiving blessings from heaven. Learn to give freely. There is a very powerful spiritual energy behind empowering others to acquire wealth and abundance.

As you continue to empower others to fulfil their destinies, you attract invisible helpers (Angels) to yourself. Getting things done will become much easier for you. Invisible doors leading to divine opportunities will be opened.

Empowering others is walking in line with divine purpose. God created you to help enhance the quality of life of others. This is the true meaning of life, but many have forgotten their primary purpose in favor of another agenda. Anything outside love and helping others is purely selfishness, and selfishness is dangerous.

Selfishness

The dangers that accompany selfishness may not be apparent to the natural mind, but the evidence of these dangers is tangible. Selfishness repels favor, hinders opportunity, slams shut the window of heaven, and deters divine help.

The world is in great chaos today because of selfishness and greed. The political unrest and the callous murders of human beings in the Middle East and other parts of the world today is an obvious manifestation of how selfishness has overtaken people's minds. Out of greed, bigger nations want to control the resources of weaker or smaller nations. We cannot deny the fact that greed engenders cynicism, fascism, and animosity between people and nations.

To enjoy peace, favor, and tranquility, you must have empathy for those in need. Help the needy, the widows and the fatherless.

The characteristics of selfishness are the malady we see all over the world today. Crime has taken over the world, life is no longer safe, and young people are becoming gang members to fulfil social norms. Government spending on security has quadrupled in the last decade as we vainly attempt to reduce crime yet crime is on the increase.

To enjoy peace, favor, and tranquility, you must have empathy for those in need. Help the needy, the widows and the fatherless.

"Learn to do well; seek judgment, relieve the oppressed, judge the fatherless, plead for the widow" (Isaiah 1:17).

Blessings result not necessary from hard work but from favor. When you remember the poor and reach out to them in love, you are defining an atmosphere with an open, spiritual connection between heaven and yourself. We live in a world where everything functions by cause and action. We reap what we sow.

Do Not Hold Back

Holding back other people's benefits or rewards is a catalyst to wretchedness, poverty, and lack. When you hold back what will benefit others deliberately, when you are supposed to give it, you may cause pain to the receiving soul, and this will result in the creation of a negative spiritual atmosphere, thereby attracting divine wrath.

It is nothing but a snare to deny people who have provided services for you what they are due.

It is nothing but a snare to deny people who have provided services for you what they are due. Sometimes we call people to mow our lawn because we know they are desperate and in dire need of money. Some underpay them, taking advantage of their desperation. This is wrong and can hinder your progress, because you are using a dishonest scale. Nothing is wrong with bargaining, but do not exploit others or take advantage of their desperation.

If you are an employer and want your business to thrive, you must take this principle seriously. Pay your staff what they are due at the right time, because they have provided a service and deserve a wage for their labor. It is immoral to violate the "pay for work" principle, and such violations have the capacity to incur a curse that will deter blessings.

Be nice to those who work for you. Pay them a salary commensurate to the work they have put forth and comparable to the pay for similar jobs in your area. Occasionally, buy presents for your staff, and once in a while, take them out for dinner at your expense. This act will not just bring about staff motivation and increased productivity, but will also release abundance and has great spiritual implications. Such actions open heaven and pave the way for greater opportunities.

Keep Your Promise

Not keeping promises is another violation of the law of abundance. People make promises and fail to keep them, assuming that it is common business ethics. There is a common saying that, in the business world, it is permissible to be a little bit dodgy in your dealings. The saying is common because it represents an accepted norm.

This concept may be convenient for many, but it has serious negative effects spiritually. The divine is fair and will not discriminate. The life will give you back what you sow to it seven-fold. When you cheat others to acquire material gains—even though your actions may appear logical, reasonable, or customary—you are bound to receive the same thing in return in a ripple effect. Be conscious that you cannot avoid reaping what you have sown. That is the law.

Stewardship

Our primary assignment on earth is one of a stewardship. We are to make this world a better place to live by supporting one another in every way we can. Understanding this truth will help you to engender an invisible spiritual atmosphere that will allow you to open a portal for wealth and abundance.

From our own natural experiences, we can deduce that one life depends on others. In other words, you need me just as much as I need you. This is the divine order, and it cannot be broken. I think this phenomenon is best described as follows: our lives are connected, and we should be quick to share in each other's burden. We often hear the words "be thy brother's keeper." This advice may be difficult to assimilate because of those who have hurt us without just cause. But being hurt by others is away a way of life.

Sometimes people will lie to or about you, say horrible things about you, insult you, and treat you as if you are nobody. You cannot avoid these common pains of life. Jesus said, "Offense will come . . ." People will offend you and mistreat you, but you have already been told by the Master that all this will come: "But be of good cheer for I have overcome the world." Sometimes pains are meant to strengthen us and prepare us for the next step. We should not see pain as God punishing us; it is not in His nature to reprimand with pain. God's nature is pure love.

Let's illustrate this concept further. You need me to live a harmonious life. This principle is often referred to as divine exchange. I need what you have, just as you need what I have. For example, you need other people to be your friends, to teach your children at school, to provide emergency help in an accident, and to build the house to live in. You need other people to produce your food, your clothes, and virtually everything you need to physically survive. Likewise, others need what you have for subsistence. Even if you have all the money in the world, you need people to accept it in exchange for goods and services; otherwise, your money would be worthless. Imagine a world where you are all alone. Imagine the inevitable loneliness, boredom.

> *The more people you have around you, the more people who accept you, the more people want what you have, the more wealth and abundance you will command.*

The more people you have around you, the more people who accept you, the more people want what you have, the more wealth and abundance you will command. You have probably heard of the law of the *large number*. In a business world, the more customers you have, the more the profit. Many people have made millions from social media because of the large number of followers they have. This suggests that you are who you are because of others. People's perception about you can alter your destiny positively or negatively.

You must consciously bear in mind that you live because of the person next to you, and they also live because of you. No man is an island. You cannot live by yourself; for life to be meaningful, you need relationships with others, such as your family members, your neighbors, residents of your community, and citizens of the world at large. How you treat these relationships is important.

Cherish and respect these marvelous relationships by sincerely loving others. Love is demonstrated by sharing in others' pains and joy. This can only be achieved if you understand that the well-being of others is also your well-being.

As a steward, you must be conscious that you own nothing: you came to this world with nothing, and you will leave at death with nothing. Holding on to material things is mere foolishness, but this idea still subsists among unenlightened souls. The inclination to acquire money, live in a big house, drive flashy cars, wear expensive clothes, sample the finest cuisines, and so on is normal, but it is abnormal to close your eyes to the suffering of others. Neglecting this spiritual law of stewardship is declaring war on your own soul.

If you were so self-centered that you could not feel the pain of those suffering hunger and thirst, you would be gloomy and despondent. This is a common phenomenon in the world today. In the western world, we are busy amassing wealth and striving toward living superior lives, binning tons of foods that we cannot consume. What a waste! Meanwhile, our neighbors, especially children, in third-world countries in Africa and Asia are starving to death due to a lack of food. A large number of people are dying daily from thirst, lack of good medical health facilities, and poor educational facilities—and we are not bothered. Where is the love God spoke about? This is all selfishness and despondency, which bring weariness to the soul and eventually deter blessings and abundance.

A good steward is one who shares in the pain and grief of others, has the true nature of God, and reaches out to those in need. A good steward knows that what he possesses was given to him only so he could help others who genuinely need it the most; he is conscious that everything he owns has been placed in his custody as an administrator.

This is the spiritual truth: you take nothing with you when you die. The only gain that can be attributed to you after your life on earth is what you have done in love for humanity, because these actions bring blessings and abundance that transcend this life. The money you left in your bank account or the number of house you left behind won't matter.

Remember that we will all stand before our God to give an account of how we lived our life here on earth and what we have done to touch people's lives. This is a judgement you can cannot avoid.

Steps I Must Take to Change My Thinking to Live in Divine Health and Attract Favor

1) To live a prosperous life and enjoy divine health, I must strive to think positively, knowing that what I consistently think of, I attract.

    Finally, brethren, whatsoever things are true, whatsoever things are honest, whatsoever things are just, whatsoever things are pure, whatsoever things are lovely, whatsoever things are of good report; if there be any virtue, and if there be any praise, think on these things. (Philippians 4:8).

2) To attract divine favor and walk beneath open heaven, I must reach out to the needy, the orphans, and the widows.
3) By helping others to succeed, I am opening divine doors for my own success.
4) The divine is fair and does not discriminate. It will give back to me whatever I have sown, so I must be conscious of how I treat others.
5) Just as I need people to live, people need me to live. So I must respect, cherish, and love people. This is true love.
6) I am aware that I will stand before the Maker of the universe one day to give an account of how well I managed the resources put in my

care. Therefore, I consider it a responsibility to make sure I reach out to the poor, the widowed, and the orphaned in the best way I can.

7
Affirmation

Affirmation allows you to unconsciously create the atmosphere that will give birth to your desire in the unseen world.

What you say is very important in bringing about the desires of our heart. This law was mentioned already in chapter 3, when we looked at the desires of your heart. Your heart has a significant role to play in receiving divine blessings. The powerful thoughts of your heart have the potential to bring about what you dwell on consistently over a significant period of time. This is how affirmation works. When you desire a thing, you should create the atmosphere spiritually in the invisible realm for your desire to take form through confession. Affirmation allows you to unconsciously create the atmosphere that will give birth to your desire in the unseen world. In other words, what you believe is created in the spirit realm. Even when your thoughts have given form to your desire, there are other key factors that you put to work to engender the physical manifestation of your desired result.

Key Factors

When you sincerely desire something in your heart for a long time, your thoughts will spiritually give birth to your desire.

Because your thoughts have taken form in the spirit realm, you can get what you believe in the physical realm if certain factors are engaged. You must apply other key factors to experience the physical manifestation of your desired blessing. This is where affirmation plays an important role. When you sincerely desire something in your heart for a long time, your thoughts will spiritually give birth to your desire.

The next step is to apply the force of affirmation by making positive confessions or openly declaring that you have what you desire. For instance, if you seek employment, start declaring that you are employed, that the job is yours. The force of affirmation is the vehicle that merges the invisible with the visible. It is best seen as the means that gives you access to the spirit realm and allows you to collect what you have formed through your thoughts and desires in the physical realm. This can be referred to as simply creating a bridge between the spiritual and physical realms. What you say is very important, hence you must declare your desires consistently, boldly, and openly. Say them to your friends, declare them to yourself, repeat them upon waking. Tell people that you have received what you desire. This may sound like empty boasting or building a castle in the clouds, but do not relent in your declaration. You are preparing the atmosphere that will facilitate the manifestation of your desires. Eventually, you will experience blessings and abundance. It is like gathering clouds. When the cloud becomes heavy, rain falls.

Negative Affirmation

Just as there are two sides to a coin (the head

and the tail), we have both positive and negative affirmation. Many people are sick, poor, and rejected, because they consistently if unconsciously hold thoughts of sickness, poverty, and rejection. Negative affirmation is very subtle. Many people believe that by saying negative things have happened to them, they will attract sympathizers. This may be the case, but it only worsens their situation, because the divine does not discriminate. Just as the sun gives equal light to both the kind guys and the bad guys, so do you become the victim of what you desire and confess with your mouth. This law, which cannot be broken, says, "Your heart's desire shall be granted and you shall have what you say."

If you hang around the poverty-stricken people, you will easily be able to deduce why they are poor through their mentality and confessions. Likewise, when you hang around the rich and affluent, you will also be able to tell why they have abundance in life through their positive mental attitudes and confessions. Your confession is simply a portal that allows good or bad to come to you.

Vague Desires

There are many who fall in the category of people with mediocre minds. These people cannot actually identify or create a definite desire because they are never sure of what they want in life. A typical example would be someone who wants to be a medical doctor today but tomorrow wants to be a classroom teacher. Inconsistent in their desires, these people want too many things at the same time and end up having nothing. The Bible refers to them as *double-minded*. This type of mind will exclude you from receiving blessings and abundance. When you ask what they are striving for, they will often reply, "I am not quite sure."

Negative thoughts and affirmations can cancel positive ones. Positive thoughts can be likened to still, clear, pure water in a river. When you look down at the water, you can see your image clearly. When you entertain negative thoughts, it is as though you've poured dirty water into a once-pure river. They will make your vision blurry and muddied.

Some people start with definite desire and positive affirmation but find it difficult hold on and so give up when their circumstances become difficult. They allow their thoughts to waver based on what they see with their eyes or what they hear with their ears. But spiritual things do not conform to a physical outlook. In short, they act to the contrary. You cannot measure spiritual things with physical facts; they work on principles. You must adhere to the principles of how to receive what you desire regardless of what you see around you.

Physical Senses

When you rely largely on your understanding of how things seem to work in the physical realm, you will completely lose your sense of your spiritual nature...

Your physical senses enable you to have contact with the physical realm, and they cannot function within the spirit realm; in fact, they oppose it. When you rely largely on your understanding of how things seem to work in the physical realm, you will completely lose your sense of your spiritual nature, which is, in fact, your true self. Just as you have your physical senses to function in the physical realm, you have also been given spiritual senses that allow you to function as a spirit being. All things in the physical realm are temporal and subject to change. For example, being broke today does not mean you will not be rich tomorrow; being sick today does not suggest that you will not be well tomorrow. The circumstances you may be in today are not permanent, and they are subject to change if the appropriate force is applied.

Things in the spirit realm are more real than those in the physical realm. To gain access to things in the spirit realm, you must put your spiritual senses to work by spending time in prayer and meditation.

Steps I Must Take to Enjoy the Abundance I Desired

1. I must be aware that negative affirmations can deny me true abundance. Therefore, I must constantly dream of great things and bring them into physical existence and manifestation through positive affirmations and confessions.
2. Irrespective of the difficulties I may be experiencing right now, I must believe I can change my circumstances for the better by positively declaring what I desire.
3. To experience blessings and wealth, I must be preoccupied with positive affirmation by declaring consistently that I am rich, blessed, and living a life of abundance and peace.
4. I must do my best to avoid people who have negative views of life.
5. I must surround myself with people who have a positive attitude toward life and are not afraid to take calculated risks, rather than hanging around those who never attempt to change their circumstances.
6. I must believe that my desires will come to

pass if I confess them daily.

7. I must consistently remind myself that I will have what I say, whether good or bad.

8
Faith

The final aspect we will look at is faith. From the ancient times until now, several attempts have been made to define faith by various religious sects across the globe. This suggests to us how important faith is in relation to human existence; therefore, it should not be ignored.

However, the most remarkable definition of faith is found in Hebrews 11:1:

"Now faith is the substance of things hoped for, the evidence of things not seen."

This verse affirms that the ability to see beyond the natural realm into the spirit or invisible realm to lay hold of something you desire is what makes you triumph in life and command abundance. A man of faith believes nothing is impossible if he sets his mind to it. This ability to believe is very common among those who can see the future and set the law of faith in motion through hope. The law of faith suggests that what you can imagine, you can gain, if you believe that you have received it. The only way you can receive anything meaningful in life is to first see it and reach out by faith to get it.

...faith is taking appropriate steps to attain what you believe in your heart while doubting nothing.

There is a common adage that says, "What you see is what you get." I believe that this saying with all my heart. Abundance is as simple as this: if you can see it, you can have it. What you get begins with what you can envision, and what you can envision sets the law of faith in motion, facilitating your receiving.

Some people see faith as believing and some as acting. On this note, I will define faith as not only believing but also acting on what you believe. Simply put, faith is taking appropriate steps to attain what you believe in your heart while doubting nothing. In chapter 7, when we looked at affirmation, I said that once you desire anything, you must back up your desire by proclaiming that you have already received what you want. This is a manifestation of your faith, and faith is the force that allows you to retrieve what you have created in the spirit realm through a sincere desire in the physical realm. Let's illustrate this with couple examples:

1. Your desire is to get a job and you have been declaring that you have got the job. The act of actually going out to start looking for a job with a strong conviction in your spirit will definitely lead to you finding a job; the act of searching is, therefore, an act of faith.

2. You may be thinking of starting your own business. The acts of writing a business plan, carrying out market research, going out to seek advice from experts, renting an office to commence the business, and believing that the business will succeed are demonstration of faith.

From the above illustrations, we can conclude

that faith is the supernatural force you need to bring about the tangible manifestation of something you desire. Faith is believing that what others see as impossible is possible. We can sum this up with few classic examples.

A man was diagnosed with cancer, and the doctor confirmed that he had only a short time to live. The man knew that if he did nothing about the diagnosis, he would die. When he got home, he searched the Bible for scriptures that promised him healing. He wrote out those scriptures in a notebook and began meditating on these verses, confessing them day and night, and claiming his healing. I was told he confessed the scriptures countless times, praying and fasting, and that, eventually, the infirmity of cancer left him and he received his desire.

I heard another story of a husband and a wife who had a car accident. The wife suffered a more severe injury in the accident than her husband, but the husband believed that he was going to die and told himself he was dead; meanwhile, the wife kept saying she would survive and not die. In the end, she actually survived the accident, and her husband died because of what he had proclaimed.

From these examples, we can obtain that your circumstances are not what determine your ultimate result, rather your confessions and faith are what create your life experiences. Your fortune and misfortune in life are what you have sincerely believed will happen. By having this understanding at the back of your mind, you can begin writing a new chapter in your life; you need only to change your beliefs and your confessions.

Regardless of what you are going through right now, know that the situation is temporary – change for the better is coming. The fact that you don't have money in your bank account today does not mean you will never make money in life. We have all heard of the description "rags to riches." Many people are trapped in terrible situations today because of what they believe, think, and say about themselves. Your life is in your own hands.

No matter how tough the problem you are going through right now, you can change it through faith. Remember that there will always be a sun rise after every night – "Weeping may endure for a night, but joy cometh in the morning" (Psalm 30:5). Faith is not believing in the best today and changing your mind in disbelief tomorrow – "A double minded man is unstable in all his ways" (James 1:8). Faith is an absolute conviction and total trust in the promises of God about any situation. This is the force that commands blessings and abundance.

Faith Is a Lifestyle

We are divinely wired to live lives of faith.

What we do, what we say, and what we think must be faith-based. Our foundations must be built on faith and faith alone — "The just shall live by faith" (Habakkuk 2:4, Romans 1:17, Galatians 3:11 and Hebrews 10:38). Anything done outside faith is done in fear and can be dangerous, because in fear, you are living contrary to the way divinely prescribed. Only a life of faith is pleasing unto the LORD — "But without faith it is impossible to please him" (Hebrew 11:6).

Interestingly, nothing you do, except exhibiting faith, can please God. Living a life of faith places divine confidence and trust in the supreme ability of God to provide for you by meeting your needs and protecting you according to His promises — "For all the promises of God in him are yea, and in him Amen, unto the glory of God by us" (2Corinthians 1:20).

> *Nothing is as glorious as living a life of faith.*

Nothing is as glorious as living a life of faith. The only person the devil dreads is a man or woman of faith. The devil can conquer only the person who loses faith in a troubling time — "If thou faint in the day of adversity, thy strength is small" (Proverbs 24:10).

So, don't give in to the devil. Stand your ground, resisting the devil by faith, and he will flee from you. You can do this by resting absolutely on God's message concerning your life and ignoring the devil's lies. He will try to convince you that God is not capable of keeping His word, because he knows if he can get you not to believe the word of God, you will not be pleasing God. When you cease belief in God, you implicitly say, "God, I don't believe you are all that powerful, and neither do I trust you to keep your word. I think the devil is right." Guess what? You are effectively telling God not to bother protecting you. You're saying you'll go with the devil on this. Remember that the devil is a thief, and "the thief cometh not, but for to steal, and to kill, and to destroy" (John 10:10)

Failure to have faith in God makes you vulnerable to becoming a victim of the devil. It is like giving a ticket to the devil to come and steal your finances, destroy your destiny, and kill all those who you love. But Jesus said, "I am come that they might have life, and that they might have it more abundantly" (John 10:10). You can access this glorious realm of abundant life Christ offers only through faith. Faith in what? Faith in God and the finished work of Christ at Calvary.

A man living a life of faith can never fall short of the glory of God, because living a life of faith is consistently trusting and depending on God, not on our own human strength. The error many make today is trusting on their own strength— "For by strength shall no man prevail" (1Samuel 2:9). In spiritual matters, human strength is inferior; reliance on it is futile and wearies the soul. Human strength includes a man's physical strength, mental strength, and human understanding. Our battle is not against human beings but against invisible forces in the spirit realm far superior to the strength of a million humans put together. Our reliance on supernatural (divine) power is what ensures our success in the race of life. Faith in the sovereignty of God's power gives us dominance over invisible forces in the spirit realm militating against our success.

Faith in the sovereignty of God's power gives us dominance over invisible forces in the spirit realm militating against our success.

Faith is the only superior weapon of warfare at our disposal to ward off evil forces that oppose our blessings and abundance in life.

You may think that you do not have faith, but this is not true; you were created with some form of faith in you. Going to bed and sleeping at night with the belief that you will wake up in the morning is an act of faith. The ability to wait for your salary at the end of the month is faith. The ability to pick up the phone and call your friend to tell him you'll see him later, not thinking of potential accidents or other factors that might make it impossible for you to arrive there, is faith. You can gather from the few instances I gave that you have some form of faith. This kind of faith is inherent in man, and it is called the natural faith.

Natural Faith

Natural faith takes root in the human brain by relying purely on our mental assent. This is the innate faith in every man. It accepts suggestions from our brain by drawing strength from things around us and applying our physical senses, which function on what we see, hear, feel, smell, taste, and touch. It is somehow attached to our mental ascent and functions more with our brain than our spirit. Natural faith is very important and should not be neglected. It is as important as the next aspect of faith we will be talking about in the following section — the supernatural variety.

Natural faith allows us to contact and interact with our physical world. It permits us to navigate our daily lives, relate with family and friends, go to the supermarket and believe that our money will be accepted as a medium of exchange for payment of the items we have purchased. When you wake up in the morning, you can predict with utmost certainty whether it will be a sunny or rainy day based on how the weather looks. Kids believe what their teacher tells them at school is the absolute truth. All these are examples of natural faith.

This type of faith is available to everybody, but we still have the ability—called the right of choice—to accept natural faith as the truth or to reject it. For instance, you have the right to accept the news you hear on your television as the truth concerning a matter, or you have the right to reject it as a lie.

Predictable and routine, natural faith allows you to determine the likely outcome drawn from experiences or the general societal norms. This is what society considers to be right. Most people who claim to have faith are referring to this kind. This brings us to the concept of supernatural faith.

Supernatural Faith

This variety is dependence on the supernatural ability of God to meet our needs. This type of faith does not give us the opportunity to depend on our mental assent but depends solely on a higher deity and is far superior to our natural faith. This is the faith we must live by if we are to command blessings and abundance in life. Genuine faith is not acquired in the realm of the intellect or fathomed by human brain, but it is far more that. It is a spiritual force that enhances our ability to look beyond the natural realm, see into the spirit realm, and reach out for things we cannot normally achieve with our own human strength; it relies strongly on the promises of God and not our mental assent.

Supernatural faith is the faith you conceive in your spirit. It transcends our natural understanding into the supernatural realm and hopes for what you perceived in your spirit based on God's promises in His word. Being convinced and persuaded by supernatural faith, you are not deterred by any circumstances but rather hold on to your expectations, not wavering in thoughts, words, or actions.

This kind of faith is absolute and is ingrained in your spirit. It is considered as the absolute truth about a matter, even though it has not yet physically materialized. We can refer to this type of faith as an absolute trust in God for everything. Supernatural faith believes the Word of God is the only truth. This could be likened to anxiously expecting rain in a drought.

When you achieve this level of faith, you become a supernatural being because you have transcended from the natural understanding into the realm of God. There is nothing you hope for that you will not receive by exercising supernatural faith— "...with God all things are possible" (Matthew 19:26).

Supernatural faith is an assurance that sincere desire will come true. I mentioned in chapter 7 that when you desire a thing intently, it takes form in the spirit realm. However, you need faith to transform desires from the spirit to the natural realm. Therefore, faith can be seen as the bridge between the spirit and the natural realms. It grants you access to the spirit realm, where you can obtain your desired blessings and abundance. Supernatural faith can be referred to as a creative faith, in the sense that it brings what is in the unseen world into the visible realm, because you have the ability to function both as man and spirit. This is possible because man is a three-dimensional being. This is discussed further in the next section.

Steps I Must Take to Set Faith in Motion

1. The word of God must be the standard for my faith.
2. I must always search the scripture to find the right promises of God for what I am believing for. For example, if I need healing I must look for the scriptures on healing and claim it for my healing.
3. I understand that without faith it is impossible to receive anything from God and I also know that supernatural faith only "...comes by hearing, and hearing by the word of God" (Romans 10:17). So, it is important that I must, listen to messages, read and meditate on the word of God, in order for my faith to grow.
4. I will pray when I desire anything and believe that I have received what I prayed for, doubting nothing.
5. I can achieve anything if I can muster the faith to receive it.
6. All things are possible and achievable as long as I have the confidence to make them happen.

9
The Three-Dimensional Being of a Man

The spirit aspect of a man is what makes him a divine being...

Man is a spirit. He has a soul and lives in a body. The spirit aspect of a man is what makes him a divine being and allows him to contact invisible realms. The spirit gives life to man and upholds the soul and the body together in harmony. Without the spirit, the body is dead. Death is a lifeless state, and occurs when the spirit of a man is absent from his body. When we say someone died, it means the vital force (the spirit) that sustains life in a body has departed. Although the spirit of a man is invisible and cannot be seen with our physical eyes, yet it plays a significant role in the soul and the body.

Many people believe the soul and body are the only important dimensions of a man, and that the spirit is less important. This is why some will spend a huge amount of money and time to acquire intellectual knowledge that will help to enhance the functionality of the human mind and interest in physical appearance, while doing little or nothing to enrich our spirit, which is far superior to our mind and body. It is ignorant to look after our body and neglect our spirit, because the spirit is the life of the body.

When the spirit departs at death, the spirit lives on, but the body is left behind to be thrown away as garbage. The spirit of a man never dies; it simply leaves upon death. The spirit is the life force placed in man by the Creator. But we will not be discussing what happens to the spirit of a man at death in this book.

Often, the terms *soul* and *spirit* are conflated. Secondly, the heart is sometimes used to represent the spirit or the soul. In the truest sense, the heart of a man is actually the spirit of a man. It is completely different from the physical heart that pumps blood to the body. We have two types of man. One, a spirit man and two, a carnal man. A carnal man is a man who is ignorant of his true nature—his spirit. He cannot discern spiritual things because he considers them needless or even foolish. He prefers to exert energy on what he can see and perceive with his natural senses over giving reasonable consideration to his spiritual nature.

A natural man cannot see beyond his bedroom's four walls and, yet, he is predominantly occupied with what he can see, feel, touch, hear, taste, and feel. A natural man is interested only in what he can see right now. His thinking and actions are largely influenced by his physical environment. This is demonstrated by how he reacts to lies that others around him believe to be the truth. For instance, lies like news and rumors conveyed by the media. A lie is anything that contradicts the truth (the spirit). A natural man seeks evidence and needs to be convinced of spiritual truths, which he despises. On the other hand, a spiritual man possesses deeper insight into spiritual matters and takes advantage of his spiritual understanding to attract abundance and blessings to his life.

The spirit controls the physical. There is an

old adage that states that "a one-eyed man is a king in the congregation of a thousand blind men." Likewise, a person with any form of spiritual insight can control many who are spiritually naïve.

Man has the inherent ability to seek one form of power or another. This is the true nature of a man—spirit seeking expression. This power is often abused by the blind and the unenlightened mind. Think, for instance, of most third-world countries, where a president of a nation takes over the government by force when not elected and attempts to rule and dominate his subjects with fear and tyranny. Some exercise their power through diabolical and other negative means. This obviously embodies the dark side of the of the spirit realm, which will not be covered in this book, since our focus is purely on abundance and blessings.

People today use words without actually knowing their true meaning. For instance, the statement "poor spirit or poor soul" is often used to describe someone going through difficult times or problems. This is often true when viewed from the spiritual dimension. The hardship people experience in the natural dimension reflects their suffering in the spirit.

It is spiritually suicidal to neglect our spiritual nature at the expense of our carnal nature. When armed with an understanding of the superiority of the spiritual nature of man over our physical nature, we can avoid the spiritual suicide connected to neglecting our spiritual-self. The Bible says, "For to be carnally minded is death; but to be spiritually minded is life and peace" (Romans 8:6). The lack of understanding of your spiritual nature and authority, and too much reliance on your mental ability at the expense of your spiritual well-being are grave errors, as they could have serious consequential effects on your life. Unfortunately, this is the category many find themselves in.

Our society today focuses only on the need to enhance our mind and mental well-being to acquire educational knowledge and understand our physical environment to meet our material needs, which have evolved around humans' basic needs. But nothing is said about our spiritual well-being.

This societal expectation has become a generally accepted norm from one nation to another. This expectation has become so widely promoted and accepted as a way of life that it has also filtered into our family fabric. The onus for parents to bring up their children educated has been heightened. Nonconformity to this societal norm is deemed taboo. As a result, a great proportion of parents today are too concerned about their children's educational performance at school. This shift in perception has geared family's spending toward the development of their children's mental capacities to help them excel in this aspect of life, and yet little or nothing is done to help them develop the spiritual aspect of life. This is carnal and will ultimately result in spiritual death.

Basic human needs, as defined by Maslow in his Hierarchy of Needs, are survival, security, belonging, importance, and self-actualization. These needs cannot actually be realized when a man's spirit-being is weak. Only when a man has attained a harmonious state in the tripartite spheres of life — which consist of spirit, soul, and body — can his human needs be met in the true sense. Otherwise, all efforts to enhance our mental and physical image comes to nothing.

A sound spirit is a sound body. Likewise, an impoverished spirit is an impoverished body. True joy comes from within, not from external sources. Many look around widely — for money, for entertainment — for what can make them happy. The entertainment industry has become a money-spinning machine because the world is spending a fortune in an attempt to obtain joy. The quest for satisfaction and bliss has driven many to alcohol consumption, drug use, and more. Any happiness obtained from external sources is empty and does not last long.

True joy is a function of the soul — from within. It is a complete waste of time to seek true happiness from other sources. We must understand that true happiness comes only when we are able to maintain a balance between the tripartite nature of our being. Any imbalance in our spirit, soul, or body will lead to an inharmonious state and result in discomfort in our soul. Discomfort in the soul will bring pain and unhappiness. Trying to buy happiness with our money is only temporary, and the desired happiness will not be achieved not until we find ways to balance the imbalance between our spirit, soul, and body. It is only then that we can attain true bliss. Jesus said "Come unto me, all ye that labour and are heavy laden, and I will give you rest" (Matthew 11:28). Purest form of rest can only be found in Jesus.

Where Does Faith Come From?

What you hear and how you hear it plays a significant role in your faith walk.

Faith is activated by what we hear. "So faith cometh by hearing, and hearing by the Word of God"

(Romans 10:17). What you hear and how you hear it plays a significant role in your faith walk. When you hear the Word of God over and over, it streams down to your spirit and begins to take root in your heart. Once the word gains entrance into our hearts, it takes root. This is the finest conscious state we can attain to be able to demonstrate faith in various capacities. Our faith is enhanced by what we hear. Hence, it is important that we guide against what we hear. Words of discouragement and fear will impair our faith.

However, living a life of faith is a choice. You have the right to choose whether you want to live a life of faith or a life of fear and doubts. You may say, "I have never wished to live in fear or doubt. I just kind of find it difficult to get rid of fear." Although fear is a spirit, you are the author of your fear. The fear you experience today has been developed gradually over a period of time, and until it is overcome by your will, it will dominate your subconscious mind. At this stage the spirit of fear creeps into your mind and takes total control of your ability to exercise faith in certain situations.

To live a life of faith is a choice, since you develop faith through what you allow to come into your subconscious mind in what you hear and accept as the truth. For instance, if you have never seen a gun or heard any story about the dangers of guns, you probably won't be afraid when someone points a gun at you in the street.

Consciousness of fear stems from what you have consistently heard, read, and seen. Interestingly, what you hear, read, and see is your own choice. Although you are bombarded by fear and rumors of danger daily through TV and social media, you can decide not to listen by engaging yourself in listening to things that are nourishing to soul. Your ability to avoid evil tidings is a self-volition. What you feed your spirit man with on a daily basis will eventually increase either your faith or fear. If it is through the faithful words you have been listening to, your faith will rise.

Likewise, if you have been feeding yourself with words of fear, you are bound to be the victim of fear.

Having this understanding will enable you to guide against what you choose to listen to. To enjoy a life of abundance and blessings, you should consider only those words that will help build your faith, because faith is the anchor that helps promote your well-being.

Steps I Must Take to Enhance My Three-Dimensional Being

1. I must consistently remind myself that I am made-up of three components (spirit, soul and body).
2. My faith can only be fortified by what I hear. It is my responsibility to mind what I listen to in order to keep my faith in form.
3. Just as faith comes by what I hear, likewise, fear also comes by what I hear. To build my faith walk, I must set time aside every day to listen to faith and inspirational messages.
4. True happiness can only be attained when I am able to maintain a balance between the tripartite state of my being (spirit, soul and body). I can only achieve the state of happiness through prayer, reading meditating on scriptures daily.

10

Fear: An Invisible Enemy

Many define fear as false evidence appearing real. In other words, fear is not real, but appears to be real to its victims. I believe that fear is more than just false evidence appearing real. It is a spirit and a very powerful force that acts in direct opposition to faith. To better illustrate what fear is, let's look at fear as false evidence appearing real and as a spirit. Regardless of your own personal view on faith, I want you to understand that tolerated fear can become a stronghold and eventually constrains victims to bondage if not identified and conquered.

As False Evidence Appearing Real

This school of thought views fear from an abstract vantage point. It considers fear imaginary, but acknowledges it can appear as real to anyone who chooses to believe it exists. This type of fear functions within the mind by holding negative thoughts. For instance, someone may believe that he is in danger or facing some form of danger that does not exist. This form of fear usually finds its seat in our memory based on past experiences. This type of fear, when conceived of as thoughts in the mind for a long time, primarily controls how a man thinks and reacts to a situation and his environment. This is the most common form of fear, and almost everyone living today has suffered from this type of fear.

When we hold negative thoughts for a reasonable length of time, such thoughts will take form in the invisible realm and, over time, will eventually manifest as real. Job said, "For the thing which I greatly feared is come upon me, and that which I was afraid of is come unto me" (Job 3:25).

As a Spirit

Fear is a spirit, an enemy that has to be conquered if you are to enjoy a life of abundance and blessings. Many don't know that they are being ruled by the spirit of fear, and, as a result, they risk living with fear for the rest of their lives. Just because fear is not seen and cannot be touched does not mean it doesn't exist. The invisible nature of fear makes it so subtle that many people do not realize it exists. A large number of people in the world today are victims of the spirit of fear.

Fear has repercussion and puts its victims in perpetual bondage. It functions as a vicious cycle with ripple effects that, unless broken, can continue throughout a lifetime. The danger of fear is that it puts people under, making supposedly great men paupers. The only antidote to fear is faith.

The spirit of fear is dominant. The spirit dominates and subdue the victim's spirit. Basically, everything animate and inanimate has a spirit. Rivers (the marine spirit) have spirit. The air (spirit of the air), mountains, and rocks have spirit. Trees have their own spirits. This is the reason man worships snakes, cows, mountains, the sun, oceans, and other facets of his surroundings. Any object that is worshiped is dominant over the worshipers. The spirit behind the object of their worship uses the spirit of fear to exercise control over its worshipers to be maintain absolute control.

Faith as a Spiritual Law

When the law of faith is followed adequately, you will certainly live a life of consistent blessings and abundance.

Faith is an important spiritual law that, if applied correctly, can invoke blessings and abundance. If the law of faith is to be put to work, it must be backed by some form of force, also referred to as hope. When the law of faith is followed adequately, you will certainly live a life of consistent blessings and abundance. The law of faith does not function with sight. Rather, it functions through an inner conviction — an assurance that a dream is attainable if you sincerely hope for it. Hope is an absolute belief that a desire or dream will manifest in the future regardless of prevailing circumstances. Faith is a conscious confidence that your dream will come true. This is not mental assent but confidence that surpasses human understanding, the strong anticipation of an outcome. Hope is what prepares the way for faith.

Faith is the direct opposite of fear and works in an exactly opposite way. Just as faith can engender blessing and abundance, likewise, fear can hinder blessings and abundance.

Steps I Must Take to Set Faith in Motion

1. I understand that fear creates bondage and subverts and nullifies my desires. Therefore, I must not allow thoughts of fear in my heart.
2. I must spend time listening to preaching on faith.
3. And lastly, I will feel the ground beneath my feet, the nature growing abound around me, the sun's warmth on my skin, and endless giving of God, and I will continue to give back in the best, brightest, and most positive way I know. To love, selflessly. To be light.

Printed in Great Britain
by Amazon

50480104R00086